What is it about the power of mothers' prayer? I'm not quite sure! But after reading *When Moms Pray Together*, I can easily see how God uses their prayers to achieve incredible results—not only in the lives of their children but also in their own lives. This book will build your faith in God, keep you going when there seem to be no answers, and give you strength and hope. Learn from these real-life stories of moms who persevered in prayer for their kids—and got results!

—PAUL FLEISCHMANN
President, National Network of Youth Ministries

God has always used the lives of His people as a platform for the display of His power. The stories Fern recounts put the Father center stage. Readers will get the inside story on how determined prayer releases God's provision in even the most discouraging situations. Moms will be encouraged to pray, pray, and then pray some more.

—JENNIFER KENNEDY DEAN
Executive Director of The Praying Life Foundation
and author of *Live a Praying Life*

As moms, we erupt before God in prayer, hoping that somehow our utterings will truly make a difference. Fern Nichols offers tangible proof that not only is God listening to a mother's prayers, but He is also acting in her child's life. Faithfully. Powerfully. Eternally.

—ELISA MORGAN
President Emerita, MOPS International

I cried. I smiled. I am inspired. I agreed. I am a praying mom too, and I have seen God do miracles when moms pray together. I encourage you to call your friends and then as a group read *When Moms Pray Together*. Then, get ready for God to move mountains on behalf of your children. Tell every mom you know to buy this powerful book, read, pray, and look for God's great work.

—PAM FARREL
International speaker, author of over 25 books, including best-
selling *Devotions for Women on the Go!* and *Got Teens?*

When Moms Pray Together

True Stories of God's Power to Transform Your Child

Fern Nichols
Cyndie Claypool de Neve
Cheri Fuller
Mary Jenson

 Tyndale House Publishers, Inc., Carol Stream, Illinois

A Focus on the Family book published by
Tyndale House Publishers, Inc., Carol Stream, Illinois 60188

Focus on the Family and the accompanying logo and design are federally registered trademarks of Focus on the Family, Colorado Springs, CO 80995.

TYNDALE and Tyndale's quill logo are registered trademarks of Tyndale House Publishers, Inc.

All Scripture quotations, unless otherwise indicated, are taken from the Holy Bible, *New International Version*®. NIV®. Copyright © 1973, 1978, 1984 by International Bible Society. Used by permission of Zondervan Publishing House. All rights reserved.

Scripture quotations marked (NASB) are taken from the *New American Standard Bible*®. Copyright The Lockman Foundation 1960, 1962, 1963, 1968, 1971, 1972, 1973, 1975, 1977, 1995. All rights reserved. Used by permission. (www.Lockman.org).

Scripture quotations marked (AMP) are taken from *The Amplified Bible*. Copyright © 1954, 1958, 1962, 1964, 1965, 1987 by The Lockman Foundation. All rights reserved. Used by permission. (www.Lockman.org)

Scripture quotations marked (ESV) are taken from *The Holy Bible, English Standard Version*, copyright © 2001 by Crossway Bibles, a division of Good News Publishers. Used by permission. All rights reserved.

Italics in Scripture quotations were added by the author for emphasis.

People's names and certain details of their stories have been changed to protect the privacy of the individuals involved. However, the facts of what happened and the underlying principles have been conveyed as accurately as possible.

Editor: Marianne Hering
Compiler: Cyndie Claypool de Neve
Cover and interior design by Jeff Lane/Brandango.us

Cover photographs: Butterfly: © Fletcher Fotos/Bigstock. All rights reserved.
Slide: © Comstock Images/"Singles" collection. All rights reserved.
Flower: © Jupiterimages. All rights reserved.
Mechanics: © Wheatley/Bigstock, Creatista/Bigstock. All rights reserved.
Bus: © Fotosearch/RubberBall. All rights reserved.
Trophy: © Corbis/Jupiterimages. All rights reserved.
Women: © Brand X Pictures/Jupiterimages. All rights reserved.
Graduation: © PNC-Brand X Pictures/"Adult Education" collection/Jupiterimages. All rights reserved.

Printed in the United States of America
2 3 4 5 6 7 8 9 / 15 14 13 12 11 10 09

Library of Congress Cataloging-in-Publication Data

When moms pray together : true stories of God's power to transform your child / [compiled by Fern Nichols, Cheri Fuller, and Mary Jenson].

　　p. cm.

"A Focus on the Family book."

ISBN-13: 978-1-58997-559-0

ISBN-10: 1-58997-559-6

1. Prayer-Christianity. 2. Mothers-Religious life. 3. Mother and child-Religious aspects-Christianity. I. Nichols, Fern, 1945- II.

Fuller, Cheri. III. Jenson, Mary.

BV220.W44 2009

248.3'20852-dc22

2009024275

Dedicated to my children and grandchildren
You have brought exceeding great joy to my life—more than you will ever know.
I love you way past heaven!!
May you continue the legacy of prayer.

—FN

My children and their spouses	My grandchildren
Ty and Patti Nichols	JT
Troy and Bonnie Nichols	Joshua, Jessica (Mimi), Jack
Travis and Tara Nichols	Jared, Elizabeth
Trisha and Chris Morel	Mikaila, Nathan

CONTENTS

Acknowledgments vii

Introduction: A Letter of Encouragement to Moms from Fern Nichols ix

1. Ready for Anything 3

2. From Breaking the Law to Enforcing the Law 13

3. "Mom, Why Am I So Stupid?" 23

4. The Heartbreak of Bulimia 33

5. An Infant's Struggle for Life 45

6. Calming the "Strong Willed" Storm 53

7. Life with a Drug-Addicted Teenager 61

8. Pornography Grips a Young Man's Heart 73

9. A Divine Heart Transplant 81

10. Changing Schools, Communities, and Nations Through Prayer 91

11. Prayers Laid the Foundation for a New High School 99

12. When Children Don't Bond with the Family 107

13. Unlocked: Hope for Moms with Disabled Children 117

14. Enduring a Child's Open-Heart Surgery 127

15. My Heart *Still* Sings: A Mom Faces Her Child's Suicide 135

16. Healing for Victims of Sexual Trauma 145

17. When Children and Moms Are Hurt by Divorce 157

18. Battling Spiritual Deception 165

19. The Legacy of a Praying Mom Impacts Korea 173

20. Praying for Our Children's Friends 183

21. Help for a Child Who Scored in the "1 Percentile" 191

22. The Valley of Addiction 199

23. From Prison to Peace 209

24. Taking MITI to Ethiopia 219

25. Hope for Moms of Prodigals 227

Addendum: How To Know that God Will Hear Your Prayers 233

Notes 235

ACKNOWLEDGMENTS

I want to express thanks to all the women who took the time to write their answers to prayer and send them to us. I am sad we could not publish all of those wonderful responses in this book. To the moms whose stories we included, I am grateful to you for giving us permission to publish them. I believe the stories' impact will bring hope to hurting and discouraged moms as well as strengthen the prayer life of everyone who reads this book. The fruit of this book—to bring mothers together to pray—has yet to be realized.

Cyndie de Neve: This book would not have happened without you. You are a wonder. Your wisdom, organizational talents, and editing skills became evident as you brought this project to fruition. Thank you for the joy with which you served.

Mary Jenson and Cheri Fuller: I am so grateful and blessed that you said yes to helping with the editing of the testimonies. Your professionalism, expertise, and incredible insights were above and beyond.

To Focus on the Family and Dr. James Dobson: With humble gratitude, I thank you for believing in the vision of Moms In Touch. Dr. Dobson, I was on your radio program with 12 other moms in 1988. That interview resulted in more than 24,000 responses and launched Moms In Touch International as a worldwide prayer movement. As you continued to have us back over the years, more and more mothers heeded the call to pray for their children and schools. God bless you, Dr. Dobson. God bless your family, and God bless your ministry, which is so needed throughout the world. Your parents and grandparents prayed for you, and so you are a product of generations of prayer. It works!

I am deeply grateful for my husband, Rle, who has prayed for me and supported me wholeheartedly from the beginning of this ministry. He continues to be my number one encourager and greatest supporter.

I could not have completed this book on my own. So again, I deeply thank each one who contributed. Oh, how I love the body of Christ!

Most of all, I thank my Lord Jesus Christ for His love, direction, guidance, and mighty hand on this project. He truly is the One who deserves to receive all the glory!

We will not hide [God's teaching] from their children;
    we will tell the next generation
the praiseworthy deeds of the LORD,
    his power, and the wonders he has done.

—PSALM 78:4

Great is the LORD and most worthy of praise;
    his greatness no one can fathom.
One generation will commend your works to another;
    they will tell of your mighty acts.
They will speak of the glorious splendor of your majesty,
    and I will meditate on your wonderful works.
They will tell of the power of your awesome works,
    and I will proclaim your great deeds.

—PSALM 145:3–6

If ever there was an hour in history with potential for maximum
    world harvest, it is now.
If ever there was a time when Christ's imminent return gives a
    sense of urgency to missions and prayer, it is now.
If ever there was a time when Christians could have a world-
    wide role through prayer, it is now.

—DR. WESLEY DUEWEL, Touch the World Through Prayer

INTRODUCTION
A LETTER OF ENCOURAGEMENT FOR MOMS FROM FERN NICHOLS

One beautiful September morning I hugged and kissed my two eldest sons just before I sent them off to the nearby public junior high school. Junior high—a time when "tweenagers" step out of childhood to weather the stormy seas of changing emotions, dangerous temptations, and raging hormones. I was more frightened than they were.

Oh, God, I cried in prayer, *there must be another mom who would take time to pray with me.* My thoughts turned to a mom whose daughter went to the same school as my boys. She just might be interested in coming to my house to pray. I gave her a quick phone call, and she gave a quick response: yes! The next week we had five moms in our little group praying big prayers for our children and schools. Week after week God began to change our fears to faith.

God answered my one simple, desperate prayer, and I've never been without support since. Today, thousands of moms are finding the same peace as they pray together in a Moms In Touch group.

Yes, moms just like you uniting in prayer, bringing their fears, worries, and hearts' desires to the God of the universe. "If moms only knew" is a phrase that I often hear from those women. "If they only knew the hope I have," "If they only knew the freedom from worry I experience when we pray," "If they only knew the peace I have that God will watch over my children, their friends, and their teachers."

This book was written so that you can know what happens when God intervenes in the lives of praying mothers. God brings love, comfort, and restoration to relationships. God brings healing from illness and trauma. He rescues those trapped in anger, addiction, and fear. Moms not only experience the joy of having their prayers answered, but they also find comfort in gathering with friends. When others pray for you and your family—taking on your emotional and spiritual burdens—heaven is moved, earth is touched, and change happens.

These 25 true stories represent thousands of prayers that God answered. These moms took action, joining with others in a Moms In Touch group. Through intercession—prayer on behalf of others—these women asked God to bless their children and their schools. Each mom discovered that becoming part of a prayer community was one of the most significant things she could do for her child.

We are raising our children and grandchildren in perilous times where evil assaults on every front and threatens their very lives. We cannot stand by idly and watch them be shaped by this destructive culture. If we will not pray for our children, who will?

The greatest hope I can give a mom is to assure her that God promises to hear and answer her prayers. Will He answer those prayers in exactly the way she wants? Not always—but He will answer according to His perfect will and goodness.

The first and most important prayer we can pray on behalf of our children is that they believe in the Lord Jesus Christ and become a child of God. That they realize God's unconditional love for them by sending His son, Jesus, to die on the cross, taking the punishment for their sins, and paying for their salvation with His precious blood. And because of Jesus' death and resurrection, they can experience a personal relationship with God, both now and throughout all eternity. There is no greater joy than to know that our children and their children's children will be with us in heaven.

Another unceasing prayer is that our children develop the habit of being in God's Word regularly. For it is through God's Word that the relationship grows and matures. In contrast to the times we live in, where there seem to be no absolutes, the Bible gives a solid, unwavering foundation of truth. The Word also provides instruction on how to live a godly, abundant life. God's Word gives guidance, wisdom, direction, comfort, hope, joy, and peace. Throughout the Word, God also paints a "Portrait" of Himself by revealing His character. He is who He says He is. As our children get to know Him, they will grow in their trust of Him. Their fears will turn to faith because they will trust the One they know. This commitment to Christ is a life-long process, which is why we never stop praying for our children.

As they mature, the battle for influence over their hearts and minds intensifies, especially at school with peer pressure all around them. The temptations they face are fierce: drugs, alcohol, pornography, vulgar language, self-cutting, witchcraft, blatant disregard for authority, and sexual promiscuity. Many feel alone, unloved, abused, and without value. They are in dire need of our prayers.

The time to pray for them is now—how can we not cry out!

You can come to your heavenly Father in prayer anytime, anywhere, for anything! He promises, "How gracious [I] will be when you cry for help!" (Isaiah 30:19). What an incredible privilege God has given us. Prayer is not just for a select few, for people who lived thousands of years ago, or for "perfect" people. It's available for *you*.

Praying together is vitally important. Having been raised in a church where group prayer was practiced, it was second nature to me to want a "prayer partner" the day my boys entered junior high. Little did I know that my asking another mom to pray with me would start a grassroots prayer movement for children and schools. Now moms and grandmas are gathering in the villages of Africa, the cities of New York, the forests of Central America, and the remote towns of Russia. The hearts of moms beat the same all over the world.

Praying together is God's heart—it's His command. Over and over again the Bible points out the importance of His people uniting in prayer. One of the most famous principles expressed on group prayer is in the Gospel of Matthew. Jesus said:

> Again, I tell you that if two of you on earth agree about anything you ask for, it will be done for you by my Father in heaven. For where two or three come together *in my name*, there am I with them. (18:19–20)

When we unite in prayer, there is a special manifestation of Jesus' presence. As we come together *in His name*, there will be a clear sense that Jesus is right there in the middle of it all!

When the disciples asked Jesus to teach them to pray, He taught them a corporate prayer, "*Our* Father in heaven . . ." (Matthew 6:9). And, from the very existence of the first church, prayer groups have been an integral part of that special community. When Jesus' followers gathered after He left earth in physical form and went back to heaven, they came together in prayer (Acts 1:14). Isn't it amazing that God turned the world upside down through a small group of frightened followers who prayed together?

Moms, the Word tells us:

> Two are better than one,
>> because they have a good return for their work:
> If one falls down,
>> his friend can help him up.
>> But pity the man who falls
>> and has no one to help him up! . . .

Though one may be overpowered,
> two can defend themselves.
> A cord of three strands is not quickly broken. (Ecclesiastes 4:9-10, 12)

When people who believe in Jesus unite in prayer, burdens become lighter, faith expands, hope and peace are renewed, strength to persevere in prayer increases, and a great expectancy to see God answer grows and flourishes.

My prayer is that this book would touch the hearts of succeeding generations to take prayer seriously. I would like this to be a legacy book of answered prayer that I can give my grandchildren someday and say, "Honey, the very same powerful, loving God that answered the prayers in this book is the very same powerful, loving God who is alive today and will answer your prayers."

My desire is that these pages send an encouraging message to the next generation of moms to purposefully take the time to gather with others to pray on behalf of their children and their schools. This is spiritual warfare, and it is very, very real.

The enemy is doing everything to destroy the next generation. However, I'm excited to think of mothers who will pray seriously, standing in the gap, using the Word of God to defeat the enemy. They will cry out with one voice, standing shoulder to shoulder, for God's will to be done on earth just as it is in heaven. Our prayers are the key to saving the next generations of children.

One young mom was awakened to a greater responsibility to pray when her mother died. Here's what she wrote:

> The year following her death, I felt the Lord speaking to me regarding my mother's prayer life. She was a true prayer warrior, and her prayers were felt by our entire family. I was definitely a believer in the power of prayer. And I knew the Lord was calling me to prayer in an urgent way. It was like He was saying to me, "Your mother is now with me, and she has passed the 'prayer torch' to you. It is now your responsibility to pray for your family and extended family. Your mother has left you a heritage of prayer. It is now your turn."

> Through a series of circumstances I attended a meeting that introduced me to Moms In Touch International. When I walked

away from that first meeting, I was forever changed! I knew without a doubt that this was what God called me to. In all my years of being a Christian and praying, I don't think I had ever felt the way I did as when we prayed the Scripture that day for our children. I had gained a whole new perspective on the power of prayer! After that day, I began running full-speed ahead, carrying a flaming prayer torch! I am so thankful for the heritage of my mother. Now, I am the mother who will one day pass the torch to my children.

May it be said by our children, "I am so thankful for the prayers of my mother." Mothers, this is an investment that will last throughout all of eternity. We can all leave a legacy of prayer. Jesus did!

Did you know that Jesus prayed for you over two thousand years ago? As He was praying for His disciples as recorded in the Gospel of John, He included you and me. He said: "My prayer is not for them alone. I pray also for those who will believe in me through their message" (17:20). Listen how He prayed for us throughout John 17—more than 2,000 years ago (This is truly powerful!):

Protect them by the power of your name . . . so that they may be one as we are one. (verse 11)
That they may have the full measure of my joy within them. (verse 13)
Protect them from the evil one. (verse 15)
Sanctify them by the truth; your word is truth. (verse 17)

Today, Jesus' prayers are continuing to be answered in our lives, and we can do the same for our children and grandchildren. We can leave our descendants something eternal and not temporal. Temporal things such as money, portfolios, lands, and houses all can be destroyed. But what a great privilege to leave a spiritual inheritance that can never be stolen, misplaced, or lost. What a great joy it is that we can leave answered prayers to our descendants long after we're in heaven. Our prayers live before God, and God's heart is set on them. In years to come, we can still play a significant role in the lives of our children, grandchildren, and great-grandchildren through the prayers we've prayed for them here on earth. Our prayers, prayed in the Word and in the will of God, will impact future generations.

What's so wonderful about this legacy is that we can begin anytime, even today. If our children could express their heart in words, I believe they would say, "Mom, will you pray for me?"

Will you unite with the army of moms that pray around the world to cry out to God for your children and schools?

May the pages of this book ignite your heart to heed this mandate:

Arise, cry out in the night,
    as the watches of the night begin;
    pour out your heart like water
    in the presence of the Lord.
Lift up your hands to him
    for the lives of your children,
    who faint from hunger
    at the head of every street. (Lamentations 2:19)

My Prayer for You

Loving Father,
I pray you will give the reader a greater vision for Your power released as she prays. May she know that her prayers matter, that they make an eternal difference, that the present and future are affected when she prays. Increase her faith to believe that nothing is impossible for You. May she know Your great love for her and may she trust You even when she doesn't understand what You are doing. Give her courage to gather together with other moms. And may she know that her prayers are truly the greatest legacy she can leave her children. In Jesus' name, amen.

Call to Me and I will answer you, and I will tell you great and mighty things, which you do not know.

—JEREMIAH 33:3 (NASB)

———

Prayer will be exceedingly costly to you. You may need to let God wake you up in the middle of the night to pray. . . . Becoming a person of prayer will require a major adjustment of your life to God.

—DR. HENRY BLACKABY, *Experiencing God*

CHAPTER ONE
READY FOR ANYTHING
by Connie Halfaker of California

Early in my motherhood "career" I told God, in all seriousness, that for the first time in history He must have made a mistake. I was not the right mother for my children.

When my little redheaded Dawn stopped taking naps at 12 months, it was just one more sign she was going to be one of the fast and furious. Keeping up with her took nearly all my energy. She never stopped! She wanted to experience everything—touch it, taste it, get closer to it. And then my son was born. I was constantly exhausted and at times overwhelmingly frustrated.

One morning Dawn wanted to visit the neighbor lady who gave her strawberries from her garden. I asked Dawn to wait until I changed her brother's diaper, but she went out anyway. Why linger when a strawberry was so close? I hadn't actually said she couldn't go outside, after all.

That morning, as my infant son slept and my eager toddler was once again in her room for a time-out, I sat down to pray. But instead of quietly asking God for help, I burst into tears. I couldn't do it. It was too hard. Being a mom filled me with agonizing frustration, and I was sure I wasn't supposed to feel this way.

I felt God's patient spiritual presence directing me to look in the Bible. I read these words from Psalm 127:3: "Behold, children are a gift of the LORD, the fruit of the womb is a reward" (NASB). That verse challenged, soothed, and encouraged me. It also reminded me of a plaque I'd seen that read, "Children are fragile; handle with love and prayer." From that point on, the verse and slogan became like a first-aid kit for my hurting soul.

Over the following months, God taught me that the battle was within me and about me—not about my little girl. I began to pray prayers like "God, help me both to recognize this gift You have given me and to raise her as Your gift to me." I began to see Dawn as the precious gift the Bible said she was. That was the real start of my motherhood journey.

LEARNING THE ROPES

At age three, Dawn was strong-willed, competitive, and quick to speak her mind. She demanded strength from the adults around her, but at the same time, she was tender and protective toward the weak. I was never sure what behavior to expect from her; it was life in the extreme. On one hand, she would share all her toys with her friends, but on the other hand, she'd challenge every rule I put before her. Even at her young age, I felt as if she were evaluating my competence every day.

Once at Disneyland, we stood in line at the Jungle Cruise along with 10 adult family members. Dawn had been bouncing among us, chatting with one adult, and then another. Suddenly, we realized she was nowhere to be found. Fortunately, people had noted her red hair and were able to direct us to the ride operator who had perched her on a box next to him. When I got there she looked at me with irritation, put her hand on her hip, and said, "Mom, I was looking for you!"

When I asked her why she had gotten out of line and where she had gone, she told me she had seen a stroller by a shop entrance that she had wanted to see up close and touch. I was continuously surprised by her intense desire to explore and examine. It required me to be on my toes every waking moment.

While Dawn wasn't manipulative, early on she wanted reasons for what I asked her to do or not do, and she wanted the consequences for disobedience clearly spelled out so she could decide whether to obey or not. I'd set the timer for playtime with clear instructions that when it went off, playtime would be over. She wouldn't throw a fit or whine; she'd simply figure out legitimate arguments for why she should have more time to play. It was exhausting having to explain and negotiate and follow through on nearly everything I wanted her to do.

So I began to pray, "God, help me to teach her to back off from this constant pushing against authority." As we progressed through the toddler stages,

I saw Dawn settle down a little and develop some self-control. God was answering my prayers. Little did I know that in the future she would willingly place herself under a very large authority: the military.

When Dawn was four, our family relocated to a new community. I took a part-time job as a high school PE teacher, we joined a church, and Dawn started school. With all the outward changes putting pressure on her, Dawn's inward control slipped. Her behavior again leaned toward the extreme. She wasn't defiant or deceitful but she took every opportunity to test the limits—like the season we lived in a trailer park while we built our house.

I told Dawn she could ride her Big Wheel *if she rode on the white line.* That would keep her out of the street, I thought. But the next thing I knew, Dawn was out in the *middle* of the street, her red hair shining in the sun, riding on the white lines that spelled out "25 mph." She was holding a stuffed dog under one arm, cradling a Raggedy Ann doll in her neck, and steering with one hand. "I'm on the white line," she called out to me. Yes, she was.

God was preparing me to be ready for anything with this exacting child.

A NEW WAY OF PRAYING

I was not good at praying for Dawn. My mind would wander and bounce around from topic to topic. I begged. I repeated myself. Even so, God honored my attempt. And my prayer eventually became focused: "God, please direct us and bring people into Dawn's life who will enjoy her. Let them see the good things about her and appreciate them because You created her."

I also wanted to pray for Dawn's transition to school. After a church softball game, I expressed my heartfelt concerns about Dawn to one of my new friends, explaining that I wanted God to provide "just the right teacher," someone with an understanding heart to see Dawn's potential. My friend mentioned a once-a-week prayer gathering called Moms In Touch International. The prayer time was focused on the kids and their schools, teachers, and other students.

"Where do I sign up?" I asked her.

As the school year and our MITI meetings began, I received a blessing from God. I finally learned how to effectively pray. Soon afterward God gave me another blessing. I found I fit with another group of women. Usually my friends were athletes, like me, with whom I shared physical goals. This was the first time I had women friends who focused on a common *spiritual* goal, praying for our children and their teachers. As we prayed together each week, I felt God's presence and power in my life.

Don't get me wrong. Life didn't suddenly become "la-dee-dah, life is so perfect now that we gather and pray." It was simply that our commitment to praying together brought God's strength and presence into our children's lives. It was real. He was with our children while they were away from us; He was continually at their side.

My daughter's kindergarten teacher turned out to be the most perfect fit I could have imagined, a vibrant, confident, open-hearted Christian. She delighted in Dawn's strengths and challenged her in areas of weakness. My prayers were abundantly answered by God. He did more for Dawn than I asked Him to.

PRAYER MAKES A DIFFERENCE

As the years flew by, I continued to pray with my MITI group. Some of the other moms came and went, but the focus didn't change. We prayed with determination that God would bless our children and the community schools. We knew it was making a difference because we received positive reports from Christian teachers. They told us that the schools were choosing good curricula, the school board was wisely avoiding risky experimental programs, and the administrative personnel were acting in the best interests of the children. God was also answering the personal prayers for our children. Especially mine.

At this point, I had begun teaching elementary PE at Dawn's school. Being her teacher was a unique experience. I saw how Dawn's great athletic talent as well as her competitive nature played out in a more public setting. I believe that God's Spirit put an idea in my mind and an overwhelming passion in my heart to pray for my daughter in a new and dynamic way. My new prayer became "Please, God, help her to become a whole person, not just an athlete." Once again, I found support and strength within the MITI group.

At age 11, Dawn was playing on a club soccer team that traveled all over the county. Dawn was one of the most, if not *the* most, capable player on her team. As a result, because her standards were so high, occasionally she would become frustrated with her teammates. She still had a tender heart toward her friends, but even so her competitive drive could burst through unchecked. When that happened, she was unhappy but did not realize why.

During one particular game, Dawn reached such a level of irritation that she began dishing out critical comments to her teammates left and right. I couldn't stand by and let that happen, so I approached the coach respectfully and pleaded with him.

"Please, you've got to take her off the field!" I said.

He looked at me as if I were nuts. "What for?"

"Listen to her! She's out of control. She's not being a team player."

He shook his head. "She stays. We need her out there!"

"No," I replied. "She needs to be taken off the field. She needs to learn to be a better person than she is an athlete." Then I added, "What if she's in an accident and loses her *arm*?"

As I walked back to my seat, disappointed that my plea hadn't worked, I analyzed my own words and bizarre reasoning. *Huh? Dawn was playing soccer. Why didn't I say, "What if she loses her leg?" That would have made more sense.*

GOD PROVIDES A NEW HIGH SCHOOL

We lived in a small, rural community, which is great in many respects. But, when the time came, my husband and I felt that Dawn would be more successful in a larger, more challenging high school than what our community provided. At Moms In Touch, the group prayed for me and with me. My prayer became "Please, God, direct us to the school that will shape Dawn's future in a positive way."

God's answer to this prayer came completely out of the blue. My husband, a content-with-his-job middle school principal, felt that God asked him to apply for a job in a new district. He believed he had no real chance of getting it, but he put in an application anyway. Turns out, he was the top choice for the job.

The new school district had the ideal high school for Dawn, and since she now had a parent working in the district, she was eligible to attend. Through a series of events we believe was orchestrated by God, just before Dawn's senior year my husband became the principal at the same high school.

Now, in addition to the Moms In Touch group praying for my daughter, the women prayed for my husband as the principal. I learned firsthand how God answered those prayers on behalf of the school; many crises were resolved in a peaceful way because of God's intervention.

THE COLLEGE CHOICE

When it was time for college, Dawn was recruited by several schools from across the nation to play basketball—a dream come true. Her choices ranged from the United States Military Academy (USMA) at West Point, with a commitment to serve in the U.S. Army, to Ivy League schools with East Coast adventure, to Colorado with skiing fun, to San Diego with the beach and home nearby. We knew she was always up for a challenge, and sure enough, Dawn chose to attend West Point. Our child who used to buck authority was now placing herself under the authority of the United States military.

Since she would be heading across the country to begin her summer "Beast Barracks" training only six days after high school graduation, I started praying immediately that God would bring her Christian support. Within the first three days, Dawn became fast friends with a basketball teammate, and yes, she was a Christian. This girl's mother and I would talk when we could and we would pray—long distance—for our daughters. "Please, God," I would pray, "bring Dawn spiritually close to You—whatever it takes. Help me be ready for anything."

GOD'S PLANS FOR DAWN'S FUTURE

My daughter, USMA class of 2001, became an officer in the United States Army just before the terrorist attack on the Twin Towers. She was deployed to Iraq in February of 2004. It was the perfect place for her to exercise her competitiveness as well as her heart for the weak. My prayer became "Please, God, keep her where You want her." A special Bible verse gave me daily strength as I prepared myself emotionally to support Dawn, who was now a soldier of war.

> "For I know the plans I have for you," declares the LORD, "plans to prosper you and not to harm you, plans to give you hope and a future. Then you will call upon me and come and pray to me, and I will listen to you." (Jeremiah 29:11–12)

God did ready me; actually He had been preparing me since Dawn was 11 years old and I had asked the soccer coach, "What if she's in an accident and loses her arm?"

On June 19, 2004, a rocket-propelled grenade exploded inside the armored Humvee she was riding in. My daughter gave her right arm, literally, in sacrifice for her country and the freedom of the Iraqi people.

After we received the dreaded phone call, we waited in California until she was in the air on her way to Walter Reed Army Medical Center in Washington, D.C. It was five long prayer-filled days before we could see her. The anticipation was agony, as we had no idea what to expect. But when we walked in her room, the sight of her gorgeous red hair melted my mother's heart. All I could think was how thankful I was to be in the room with her. I felt a peace that God had His hand on my little girl's life.

When Dawn awoke from her coma, I told her that people all over the world, from San Diego to Europe, were praying for her. Dawn responded, "I felt the prayers, Mom. That is how I lived. God was with me the whole time. He never left me."

GOD PAYS ATTENTION

Today I see a young woman who is *definitely* a better person than she is an athlete. That's not because she has a diminished physical capacity; she's involved in tennis, soccer, football, snowboarding, you name it. She is a better person than she is an athlete because God wasn't paying attention to her just when she was lying in a coma; He was paying attention to Dawn her whole life. Every week as the Moms In Touch group met and lifted her up in prayer, He readied her for this trial.

I was ready too. Psalm 139 tells us that God knows our child's every step. I am able to go to bed each night with confidence that the next morning God will take care of my children all day long.

Pray Together

Where can I go from your Spirit?
  Where can I flee from your presence?
If I go up to the heavens, you are there;
  if I make my bed in the depths, you are there.
If I rise on the wings of the dawn,
  if I settle on the far side of the sea,
even there your hand will guide me,
  your right hand will hold me fast.

—Psalm 139:7–10

Lord, watching our children step out into the world when we know danger awaits them may be the hardest thing we mothers do. But we know that You promise to be with them, that they are never out of Your presence, and that nothing is too difficult for You to handle! Please surround them with protection, and watch over us as well. Settle our hearts with peace and faith. We are so glad You know the big picture. Thank You. Amen.

For with God nothing is ever impossible and no word from God shall be without power or impossible of fulfillment.

—LUKE 1:37 (AMP)

———————

If our petitions are in accordance with His will, and if we seek His glory in the asking, the answers will come in ways that will astonish us and fill our hearts with songs of thanksgiving.
  —JOHN KENNEDY MACLEAN, quoted in *Purpose in Prayer* by E. M. Bounds

Chapter Two
From Breaking the Law to Enforcing the Law
by a Southwestern mom

WHEN JACOB WAS ONLY IN MIDDLE SCHOOL, HE STARTED SNEAKING OUT WITH HIS SKATEBOARD FRIENDS TO GET DRUNK.

I didn't know at the time that he just wanted my attention. All the petty arguments we'd get into over whether or not skateboarding on public property was legal were really a cry for help. But I didn't see it—not at first.

I was busy with other responsibilities. My mother had just come to live with us, and I thought it was important to always include her in whatever we were doing. Suddenly, the time I used to spend with Jacob was consumed with taking care of my mom. I feel bad now that I would reprimand my slender son with spiky bleach-blond hair for wanting to do things "like we used to."

Schoolwork was never easy for Jacob. He used to strive to excel because his friends did. But when he started hanging out with a new group, his goals changed. He aimed as high as they did—which was not at all.

Throughout those years, our days on the soccer field brought a sense of normalcy back to our family. Jacob excelled on the soccer field. Only there did I see the smile I so missed. Only there did he get the attention he craved. And, sadly, only there did he seem at home. "Soccer was my only escape," Jacob says looking back at his youth. But when he went into high school, he wasn't completing his assignments. So, even though he was excited about being handpicked as a freshman to be on the varsity soccer team at his large high school, he was yanked out of sports because his grade point average was less than 2.0.

FINDING AN IDENTITY

Jacob had always identified himself as an athlete. But now what? "Suddenly," he says, "I was trying to figure out what to claim as my identity as a high school student. I lost my social connection as an athlete. An athlete was what made my parents proud, but I couldn't play high school sports anymore because of my grades. What was my identity? I felt I had no direction. I started running into trouble with the law. I was truant, drinking, loitering. I got piercings and tattoos. I'd sneak out to get drunk. Any kind of rebellion that I could do without hurting anyone, I would try it. I was experimenting with alcohol, smoking, not going to school, and shoplifting, trying not to get caught."

During high school, Jacob started working at Walmart. There, he met a teen mom. Unfortunately, that's also where he found his new identity: a pseudo dad. He soon became involved financially in their lives, and the mom even taught the baby to call him "Daddy." As much as my husband and I tried to convince Jacob that his girlfriend was using him, he didn't see it. He had been raised in a Christian home, and he would retaliate with "Shouldn't we rescue widows and orphans?" We drew a hard line: He had to stop seeing her. That about killed him. He was so torn. He didn't know what to do. He didn't know how to get help. When my husband and I would confront him on his drinking, truancy, or other problems, he would dissolve into tears. "I don't know why I'm doing this," he'd cry.

We paid for tutoring and for Christian counseling. We already knew Jacob had attention-deficit/hyperactivity disorder (ADHD). We also learned that Jacob had a processing disorder, which is why he was only at a fifth-grade level in reading and math. The high school allowed him to sit up front in class and ask as many questions as he wanted. But what "cool guy" is going to sit in the front of class and then ask a bunch of questions? He started skipping school altogether. We found out later he would check in for his first class, then he'd leave. If he was at school, he'd give the teacher a hard time or be the class clown rather than struggle to do the work.

He came to us one night and asked, "Tell me the truth. Am I retarded?" After one career-placement test he came home excited saying, "I know what I can do! I can be a ditch digger!" He was so proud, but it broke my heart to think the only thing he felt capable of doing was manual labor. When he was younger, he had wanted to be a police officer. But he felt he would never be smart enough to pass the rigorous police academy. So he set his sights on digging ditches, instead.

Homeschooling a High Schooler

After his sophomore year in high school, we decided to pull him out of public school and teach him at home. It took a couple of hours to wake him up in the morning, and he'd say he was tired because he didn't sleep well. I found out later he was crawling out his window in the middle of the night to get drunk. But he did work hard during our homeschool time. We had been given a basic curriculum for reading, writing, and arithmetic specifically designed for struggling students. He read the first booklet and answered all the questions with 100 percent accuracy. He was so happy! "I'm not retarded!" he declared.

We had some memorable times while homeschooling. While we floated on rafts in a pool, we'd do "popcorn reading": I'd get two copies of a book, and he'd read some aloud, then I'd read some. We'd go on field trips. But all the while, he was still rebelling. Here was my only son, the elder of two children, seemingly out of control. I didn't know what to do. I felt as helpless as he did. My daughter was a good student and a great kid. Had I done something wrong with Jacob? I just couldn't figure it out.

Nor did I know how much trouble he was really getting into.

Being Introduced to Moms In Touch

During that time, I had heard about Moms In Touch International, but I didn't want to share what I felt were my parenting failures with anyone else—especially not strangers. However, God knew that's exactly what I needed. I got on my knees (something I rarely do) and asked God to make me brave enough to go to an MITI group to pray for Jacob.

That day while I was at work, a Moms In Touch leader invited me to join her group. Thinking that it would get me off the hook, I replied, "No, my daughter's a Christian and my son's homeschooled." But this woman was persistent, asking me to try her group, which prayed for young adults and prodigals, kids who had turned their backs on authority, common sense, and Jesus Christ. Then she offered to pick me up on her way.

I went with her with hesitation and nervousness. My heart was beating fast. I was worried about having to pray out loud. I thought I had to talk "Christianese," like "O Holy God, make Your Holy Spirit indwell in Jacob's heart." I quickly learned that I could just pray from my heart.

That was such a powerful time for me spiritually. I began to understand more fully who Christ is. I was moved every time another mom would pray for Jacob, even though he didn't change overnight. I'd pray very simply: "Please, Lord, help Jacob not make bad choices." And these loving women would pray specifically for his choices in drinking, relationships, school—things I never had expressed. Their insights into my son's life, without my saying a word, moved me to tears on many occasions.

The MITI group was exactly what I needed. Instead of constantly fretting about my son, I was learning to tell God about my fears through prayer, and He was teaching me that He was capable of watching over my son. I could trust Him.

During the year and a half of homeschooling, Jacob continued to have an on-again, off-again relationship with the single mom. The little baby was adorable with her big brown eyes, and he had a hard time turning his back on her. So after Jacob acquired a high-school equivalency degree, my husband and I decided it would be best to have him live with relatives in another state. That way he'd be far away from girl trouble.

REBEL LEARNS TO WORK HARD

For seven months, he lived and worked on a farm. But fitting in wasn't easy for Jacob. He now describes that time: "I was a city boy with bleached hair, tattoos, and piercings. I was still in a funk. But I learned what it was to really work, to find dignity in myself through hard work."

It has been interesting to watch God weave together all the pieces of Jacob's work history. While he was on the farm, a friend of our family offered to give Jacob a shot in his construction company. He started out digging ditches, exactly the job he had expected to receive when he was in high school. But he didn't dig ditches for long. He soon learned he was great at communicating verbally and seeing the big picture of how to get large projects completed. God revealed to him his strengths, allowing him to be in charge of a construction crew. He had a company vehicle and an office. And he discovered he had a good work ethic, something my husband and I were relieved to see. His job began to build his confidence, and he was no longer struggling to find his identity. Now he found it in his work. Still, we prayed he'd find his identity in Jesus Christ.

WANTING TO BE A POLICE OFFICER

He had several other jobs that required physical labor before he decided to pursue his dream job: being a police officer. He had slowly returned to the faith of his youth, and was starting to trust that God might be able to do something big in his life, something "immeasurably more than all we ask or imagine," as is mentioned in the New Testament (Ephesians 3:20). But could a rebellious teenager, who used to break the law, be given the opportunity to enforce the law? Only God could make that happen. Throughout this time, I had my MITI friends praying fervently for him. They prayed not only that he'd get into the police academy, if that was God's will, but that through the process, God would strengthen his resolve to follow Christ.

Reading and spelling were still a challenge for him, so he spent hours and hours practicing how to spell legal words before he even signed up to take the police academy test. "Passing the police officer test seemed like an impossible task," he told me. "I thought, 'no way.' " He took the entrance test—and failed miserably. It was sad to see him so discouraged. Yet I was surprised to see him continue to study. The test included several law-enforcement spelling words, which he knew would be a huge obstacle, as well as basic proficiency tests in reading and math. My husband and I were amazed that our son, who was once a slacker, was working so hard at trying to get into the police academy. He signed up again for the test. And failed again. But he kept studying. For the third test, I had my MITI friends ask God to intervene. And this time Jacob passed!

But Jacob's journey had only begun. Jacob still had to jump through hoop after hoop to actually be accepted as a police officer. The test was only the first step. Then they looked into his driving record, medical history, education. Each time, there was something that we thought would be an obstacle, like his previously dislocated shoulder, driving tickets, and having to endure an intimidating psychological evaluation. But we watched in amazement as God orchestrated his passing of each one. Having to rely on God and seeing Him answer prayers of MITI moms in such amazing ways strengthened Jacob's faith in God. He knew beyond a shadow of a doubt that he didn't get into the police academy by his own strength. God had intervened for him.

But when the police academy started, boy, my anxiety and doubt doubled. Jacob was reading at about an eighth-grade level, but he would be required to do college-level curriculum. And do it all condensed into six months. Once he saw the enormous books involved, he wasn't sure either. "I didn't know what the academy involved," he says. "I was required to know the penal codes, municipal codes, Spanish, sign language, CPR, medical terminology. We'd get tested once a week. If we failed a test, we were out. I was thinking, *There is no way I can do this.*"

MITI MOMS PRAY BIG PRAYERS

Again, I joined with my MITI friends and pleaded with God to help Jacob soak up the material, be successful, and find his strength in God. My husband and I panicked. But Jacob never panicked. He would dig deep and pray. And study. Almost every waking hour, he was studying. He learned to glean what was important from the text and discard what was extraneous. He knew that demonstrating competency in police reports would be crucial and that spelling would be a huge obstacle for him. So again he spent hours memorizing key law-enforcement words.

He was doing well in the academy . . . until Spanish. "I had to have 85 percent or better on the Spanish final," he said. "On the pretest, I got 72 percent. That would have knocked me out of the academy five months into it, with just one month to go. I just was not picking it up. All along we'd have to watch people pack their bags and leave crying. I thought that was going to be me."

One of my friends volunteered to tutor him in the 175 Spanish words and the 50 to 60 Spanish sentences he needed to know. I was so grateful, and I again had the MITI moms pray. After the final, the instructor made him stand up—that's usually what happens to a cadet just before he or she is dismissed. "I was white as a ghost," he said. "I thought I was going to pass out. But the teacher said to me, 'I have good news and bad news. The good news is you passed the final. The bad news is that you missed 100 percent by one question.' I ended up getting the highest score in the whole class. And I didn't know a word of Spanish, before. That was God at work."

During the academy Jacob was living at home. He ate, slept, and breathed with his big, thick books. He studied constantly. It was nerve-racking. We'd pray together every night as a family. That was such a sweet time, watching him grow in his faith, seeing him rely on God, and knowing God was at work answering prayer.

MAKING IT THROUGH

The police academy graduation was surreal. My husband and I wept. My Friday-morning prayer partner was there too with tears streaming down her face.

"It was overwhelming to think it was completed," says Jacob. "At the fifth week of the academy, they gave me a gun and riot gear. At that time I thought, *I can't believe they're allowing me to have this important and expensive gear. I'll just have to return it when I fail.* I kept hoping I would get to prove that I could do this. Then I'd hope I'd pass the test to prove I really was smart. I didn't think I would actually make it through. I didn't think I would graduate. But I did graduate and even won three top honors. I learned I wanted to lead my life in a God-honoring way.

I was ready to take the Bible more seriously. I wanted to make God not just my number one, but my only one. I can look back and see how He was working things together for good my whole life."

I Can't Stop Praying

Now that Jacob is out of the police academy, that doesn't mean I can stop praying! God has handpicked him for a career where he is in danger every day. We pray together before he goes to work. He was never confrontational as a youth. But now he must pull cars over, investigate break-ins, and work in a gang-infested area. He puts his life on the line every day, but this is all about God working through Jacob. In fact, I can honestly say that for me, as a mom, it's less scary to have him fighting crime than it was when his back was turned against God and he was sneaking around, drinking, and being rebellious.

"When I was growing up I always wanted to be a cop, but it never seemed a practical dream," he said recently. "But when I came to God, all the doors opened. Even during the journey, it didn't seem achievable. Now, every encounter I have, I try to demonstrate God through my example and lifestyle. I think this whole journey really has been about trust, about not leaning on my own understanding, knowing that I can't do this on my own. This journey has been a miracle. Really."

Pray Together

Trust in the Lord with all your heart
    and lean not on your own understanding;
in all your ways acknowledge him,
    and he will make your paths straight.

—Proverbs 3:5–6

Dear Lord,
Help each mom learn to trust that You have a plan for her children. Help her acknowledge You and "lean not" on her own understanding. Even though the path may be challenging and fearful, may she hold on to the truth that Your plans will not be thwarted, that Your paths are straight. In Jesus' loving name, amen.

Find rest, O my soul, in God alone;
   my hope comes from him.
He alone is my rock and my salvation;
   he is my fortress, I will not be shaken. . . .
Trust in him at all times, O people;
   pour out your hearts to him,
   for God is our refuge.

                —PSALM 62:5-6, 8

———

Trust God where you cannot trace Him. Do not try to penetrate the cloud He brings over you; rather look to the [rain]bow that is on it. The mystery is God's; the promise is yours.

                —JOHN MACDUFF, *The Bow in the Cloud*

Chapter Three
"Mom, Why Am I So Stupid?"
by Cyndie Claypool de Neve of California

"*M*om, why am I so stupid?" my first-grade son asked as I tucked him in for bed. "Everyone else gets done with schoolwork faster than me."

I was stunned. How could a child deemed "gifted" by so many think he was *stupid*? Trying to hold back the tears that were welling up in my eyes, I muddled through a reminder of his strengths and how God makes everyone for a purpose—and that includes our differences. We prayed, and I kissed his light brown cheek good night, but those words rang in my ears: *Mom, why am I so stupid?*

Could He Really Have Dyslexia?
"Stupid." That was the "s" word that wasn't allowed in our house, and here was my precious son saying it about himself. I asked God to show me what I should do. I knew learning disabilities ran heavily in both sides of our families, and my husband occasionally told me he thought our son might have dyslexia. In kindergarten, he struggled to recognize the difference between "12" and "21," and his teacher said he was having trouble reading.

My son? I had followed all the reigning theories on how to get a preschooler ready to read. In fact, he won the academic award in kindergarten for reading the most books. But, it turned out, he wasn't truly reading; he was reciting from memory. And as helpful as the professionals say that is for a child, it seemed to have little impact on my son.

When my sweet six-year-old labeled himself *stupid*, I couldn't ignore the issue anymore. I started researching dyslexia, reading everything I could find on the subject. It soon became apparent that b, d, p, and 9 all seemed to be the same entity to him. No wonder he had difficulty trying to read and write. But now what? If my child was feeling stupid in first grade, when his peers were barely reading and writing, how would he feel in second grade or sixth grade or tenth? Ever since he was four years old, all he wanted to do was go to "film college" to become a movie director. How could he get to college if he could barely get through first grade? How would this affect his future?

WHO WOULD PRAY WITH ME?

While the nice moms in my Bible study prayed occasionally for my son, it didn't fill the need I had for concentrated prayer about this issue. There was so much to pray about. Not only did I need to know what steps to take academically, but I also agonized over how this disability could damage the future possibilities for my creative and outgoing son, as well as how struggling in school could wreak havoc on his self-esteem. I had seen how a learning disability could shatter a child's confidence, and how looking too hard for acceptance could land a youth in the wrong crowd, causing heartache and grief. How could I help my son understand his worth in God's eyes? How could I get him past comparing himself to others to accepting himself as a unique person, created on purpose for God Himself? Our faithful heavenly Father went before us, putting together connections not only to get my son the help he needed, but also to provide me the support I desperately craved.

Most mornings I walked my son to school, and so the crossing guard and I had become friends. She was a Christian, and some mornings after the school bell rang, we would stand at the street corner and pray for a few minutes while my baby girl patiently sat in her stroller nibbling on dry Cheerios. After witnessing big construction trucks continually zip past energetic kids waiting at the crosswalk, we began urgently praying for the students' safety at the busy intersection. Soon after, the trucks were banned from driving through the crosswalks when children were going to school or heading home. God had certainly heard and answered our prayers as we stood at the street corner. How much more would God do if we had a concentrated hour of prayer each week for our children and school?

We realized we needed to start a Moms In Touch group, and we invited our friends to join us. Praying over each of our children was like salve to a wound. Each week, as we sat in my living room, we asked God to answer our prayers for our children, their friends, and the school. In many cases, the answers seemed to come quickly. Students we prayed for started attending church groups. A mom became a Christian. God was truly at work. I clung to the fact that if God was answering those requests, He must be working out a plan to help my son receive the help he needed while retaining his confidence and zest for life.

Official Diagnosis: Only the Beginning

Near the end of second grade, it was officially determined that my son had a learning disability. After a year and a half of research and trying to convince the school staff that my son needed reading assistance sooner rather than later, I was relieved to know that he was finally eligible to receive services to help his reading. I was comforted that, after all the grueling testing, the paperwork confirmed what I had been telling my son: God had given him a bright, creative brain. However, as is typical with dyslexia, the sequencing needed for reading, math, and spelling was a struggle.

The discrepancies in his scores allowed him to qualify for services, but they didn't help his confidence or self-esteem. My smiley, energetic second grader became withdrawn and sad. When I dropped him off at school, he would slowly walk up the hill to the school yard. Then he would turn around, and as I drove away, I could see his slender figure looking sorrowfully down at the car. What a contrast to the joyful little boy who used to race onto campus so he could enjoy playtime before the school bell rang.

I later asked him what he was thinking as he watched us drive off. His answer: *Mom, I just want to run down the hill and jump back into the car.* That broke my heart! I spoke with his teacher, who also was concerned. The compassionate educator started working through my son's areas of strength, starting with his passion to direct movies. The teacher asked him to film the class readers' theater. My son did all the filming and editing on a kid-friendly camera and program. He beamed as the class and teacher watched his finished production. When the movie was shown at the spring open house, even the principal was impressed. God had truly answered our prayer of returning the joy to my son's heart.

But second grade was coming to a close, and my MITI group joined with me in pleading with God for wisdom about our school choice for the following year.

Surprisingly, a hard-to-get-in charter school, with class sizes of 20 and a willingness to modify his curriculum, had room for my son. And, even more surprising, the school district's special education division approved our transfer to the charter school, allowing him to continue with the resource program at our neighborhood public school.

God even provided a local tutor who gave us better enrichment than the expensive and highly recommended reading program that was 40 minutes away. In our MITI group, I had many thanksgivings of how God provided for our needs in ways far greater "than all we [could] ask or imagine" (Ephesians 3:20).

THE PAIN OF BEING "DIFFERENT"

Still, life wasn't easy for my son. "Why do I have to go to resource?" he would ask, tears pouring from his big brown eyes and streaming down his face. "Why does everyone finish faster than me?" "Why do I have to be so different?" Life wasn't easy for me, either. The new school allowed for modifications, but it was up to me to figure out what modifications my son needed. I'd spend hours working with him on spelling, trying every creative way imaginable to help him learn his words. And he did! He'd get As on his spelling tests—but he'd misspell the same words repeatedly in his written work.

Having been a journalist and editor for years, I struggled to focus on praising his creative and well-worded prose, while ignoring all the spelling errors and letter reversals riddled throughout the page. After working for months on the word *they*, to see it spelled *thay* over and over again made me cringe, and left me feeling as if I were spinning my wheels.

My MITI group prayed God would sustain me and help me be creative and wise in my modifications of his schoolwork. But in the pit of my stomach, I could feel that nagging concern not just for his immediate educational needs, but especially for his future. My MITI group continued to pour out our hearts to God for my long-term request: that my son would have joy and confidence, knowing that being uniquely designed by God is a gift. We prayed God would protect him from the heartache and poor choices that come when a student is weighed down with the sorrow that stems from low self-esteem and a lack of confidence.

READY OR NOT, TIME FOR MIDDLE SCHOOL

The kindergarten-through-eighth-grade charter school, which allows for personalizing the curriculum, proved to be a great fit for my son. However, there were days he begged to be homeschooled so he didn't have to compare his work to anyone else's. On the first day of sixth grade, he refused to get out of the car. The school was the same. The kids were the same. And he had already met the teacher. But his confidence was shot. He didn't think he was ready for the challenges of middle school. In truth, neither did I. I prayed with him, named a lot of his friends he'd see, and told him that staying in the car just was not an option: He had to get out. "Besides," I told him, "having your mother drag you out of the car is probably not the best way to start middle school." He slumped off to line up with the other students, his curly brown hair flopping over his dark tanned face, and I prayed God would bless him mightily that day. After school he declared, "Mom, this was one of the best days ever!"

A few weeks later, he was drawn to the lead role of the Ugly Duckling in the school's fall musical, *Honk Jr.*, and decided to try out. The character sings a solo called "Different," and he deemed that his new theme song. Then he declared enthusiastically, "I am different!" There was no trace of the sorrow that statement once contained. In *Honk Jr.* the main character is shunned and picked on until he transforms into a handsome swan. My son identified with the character and worked hard to land the role. He had to sing a difficult song for the audition. If that weren't enough, he also had to read lines in front of 40 peers. I knew he wanted the role badly when I didn't hear a single complaint about having to read in public. Many MITI moms prayed for him as he tried out. And he prayed, too—even during the audition. Afterward, he told me his leg started shaking as he sang the solo, and it didn't stop until after his audition. While he sang, he prayed God would be his strength to do a good job, despite his shaky leg and the difficult notes he had to hit. God helped him persevere and showed him a tangible example of how He can be our strength in our weaknesses. When my son found out he was cast in the lead role, he was shocked at first, and then he thanked God for the many answered prayers.

During the performance, he stood in the spotlight, with the light shining on his curly brown hair, and sang: "I'm just different. I'm just different from the rest. . . . So why should being different make me sad?" What a profound picture of his young life. No matter how often I had heard him practice that song, sitting in the theater watching him all alone on the big stage singing about being different, I felt my heart break for him all over again. Others in the audience—his relatives, principal, former tutor, and teachers—expressed the same sentiment. But that was all erased as we watched the audience and students flock around him after the show, asking for his autograph and wanting to take his picture.

"He's Got a Lot of Confidence!"

After school one day in the fall, his sixth-grade teacher and I were talking casually, and I thanked her profusely for the help she was giving him in class. What an answer to prayer she was! As we watched him chatting and having fun with his seventh- and eighth-grade friends, she commented, "He's got a lot of confidence! Even the seventh-grade teacher has noticed." I was taken aback. The little first grader who once declared, "Mom, why am I so stupid?" had found his confidence—in God. Five years later, I could see the result of praying that God would protect his self-esteem.

Because of his difficulty with school, he has developed a strong, very personal relationship with God our Father. When his family's not there to cling to during class, God is. When he's stressed about taking a test, he can ask God to replace his fear with peace and joy. When he's at an audition, having to read lines, he prays God will be his strength in his weakness. "Mom, it's cool that we can pray to God whenever we want," he says. And he thanks God often, too.

Once in the middle of the day, while standing in the kitchen, he spontaneously prayed, "Thanks, God, that I didn't have any bad dreams." His little sister was curious: "Why are you praying about bad dreams?" she asked. "It's not even nighttime." But my son was thankful that God had answered his prayer for no bad dreams, and he told Him out loud, right there in the middle of the afternoon. My son has had to learn a lesson that many people don't learn until they're much older: When we are weak, *then* we are strong (2 Corinthians 12:10). And, like the apostle Paul, my son at times even thanks God for his weakness— dyslexia—so that God can be glorified in his successes.

Learning to Persevere

Over the years, God has helped my son persevere, allowing his tenacious spirit to be rewarded, just when he needs encouragement. Despite having dyslexia, my son's sixth-grade year was a great one academically, as well as socially. At the parent-teacher conference where he received his first middle school report card, I was stunned to see he had received all As and Bs. Then in May, his teacher honored him with the Achiever of the Year award for his class. At the ceremony, as his teacher sang his praises, I had to work hard not to distract the audience by bursting into happy sobs. She read a definition of achiever: "to get or attain by effort . . . to achieve victory." She explained, "I was struck by how well this definition describes him. This has been an amazing year of growth for him and much of that growth has been attained by grueling effort. He surpassed goals and pushed for independence and excellence in his work. As for sixth grade, he truly has achieved personal victory!" What a delight to share this award with the moms who had prayed for my son.

Academics may never be easy for him. Nor will it be for me as I watch him repeatedly struggle in areas adversely affected by his dyslexia, especially reading, spelling, and math. But, having seen the amazing way God has weaved together my son's past, we look toward the future with hope and joy, knowing that God has a *good* plan for his life, one to prosper him and not to harm him (Jeremiah 29:11). The boy who once cried about being different now thanks God for making him unique, and he is confident God has a spectacular plan for his life.

Pray Together

For you created my inmost being;
>   you knit me together in my mother's womb.
I praise you because I am fearfully and wonderfully made;
>   your works are wonderful, I know that full well. . . .
All the days ordained for me were written in your book before one of them
>   came to be.

—Psalm 139:13–14, 16

Dear almighty God,
May my child always find his significance in You, the creator of the universe. May he always know that You designed him for a purpose, for Your purpose, and that You can be his strength in his weakness. In Jesus' name, amen.

If my people, who are called by my name, will humble themselves and pray and seek my face and turn from their wicked ways, then will I hear from heaven and will forgive their sin and will heal their land.

—2 Chronicles 7:14

———

Move men, through God, by prayer alone.

—Hudson Taylor, *The Story of the China Inland Mission*

Chapter Four
The Heartbreak of Bulimia
by a Midwestern mom

THE ELDEST OF OUR THREE CHILDREN, BECKY IS A HAZEL-EYED, OLIVE-SKINNED TEEN, WHO TANS NICELY. WHEN SHE'S IN A HURRY, SHE THROWS HER THICK, CURLY BROWN HAIR ON TOP OF HER HEAD IN ALL SORTS OF FUN WAYS. WHEN SHE HAS TIME, SHE STRAIGHTENS HER BEAUTIFUL HAIR SO IT'S SMOOTH AND BOUNCY. SHE CAME INTO OUR LIVES 17 YEARS AGO FULL OF SPUNK, PERSONALITY, AND ENERGY. AS THE MOST STRONG-WILLED OF OUR BUNCH, SHE'S LIKE A WILD MUSTANG THAT WE'VE TRIED TO TAME WITHOUT CRUSHING HER SPIRIT. WE'VE LOVED OUR DAUGHTER, PRAYED FOR HER, AND RAISED HER TO KNOW THE GOD OF OUR LIVES—AN AWESOME, POWERFUL CREATOR ON THE ONE HAND, AND YET A GOD WHO DESIRES INTIMACY AND RELATIONSHIP WITH US ON THE OTHER.

Becky's body began to change in fourth grade. No matter how slim and cute she looked, she felt fat and ugly. Although she didn't share these feelings with me, I could tell she wasn't comfortable with her new shape because she tried to hide her thickening body under boy shorts and T-shirts. I worried about my daughter, but I didn't know what to do.

Somewhere along the way Becky had bought into some lies that took root and grew. What were these lies? That she was fat and ugly and that God had made a mistake when He created her.

When I began sensing Becky's discontent with her body, I was meeting with a small group of mothers through Moms In Touch International every other week, and we prayed about everything for our kids. In addition to that, Becky had lots of people in her life who affirmed her in every way. *Surely,* I thought, *she'll come around and things will get better.*

A CHANGE IN EATING HABITS

Middle school was rough for Becky. Her best friend moved away at the end of fifth grade, and Becky struggled to find true friends. To add to her frustration, in seventh grade her face began to break out and worsened even though we tried one medicine after another to combat it. By eighth grade she had developed some quirky eating habits, but she thinned down and seemed more confident about how she looked. Still I sensed she wasn't the person she wanted to be and that under the surface she wasn't all that happy. One time I heard her and a friend discussing what to do for the afternoon. Becky shot down every idea that her friend came up with as "boring." I wondered why she seemed unable to get excited about anything, while her friends and siblings enjoyed simple things in life. How could I make her happy? I felt helpless to change anything.

So I prayed. In my Moms In Touch group we prayed that our kids would have a deeper intimacy with Christ, live healthy lives, and make wise choices. Often we prayed that any hidden sins in their lives would be revealed so that healing could take place. I knew Becky was having a tough time with adolescence, but I had no idea that behind her smiles, Becky was hiding a harmful secret.

When Becky entered high school, she seemed to be doing well, at least on the outside. She was a good student as always, had good friends, was involved at church, and played on the lacrosse team. She definitely looked happier, but I could tell something was wrong. One day she was in the kitchen and said, "Mom, all the Christians I know are hypocrites. And so am I." Also, she began to resent a sport she used to love: "I am sick of lacrosse. It takes over my life during the season, and I never get to play just for fun," she told me after a game one afternoon.

Despite good grades and involvement in activities, Becky didn't appear to have a passion for anything—which was the opposite of how she used to be. For instance, when she was interested in horses, she read everything she could get her hands on about them, decorating her room with posters of them and dreaming of owning one someday. When her passion was ferrets, she campaigned for months for us to let her buy one of the furry critters. We were firm in telling her no, but that didn't stop her from spending hours on the Internet researching ferrets, subscribing to ferret magazines, and saving up to buy one.

THE SECRET REVEALED

Then in the spring of her ninth-grade year, I realized what was holding Becky back: She was deeply entrenched in an eating disorder.

I knew she had developed some strange eating habits, but I thought lots of teenage girls did. I watched her wipe off the gravy from her stew meat with a napkin and dissect it to remove every speck of fat. Often I opened the drawer where I kept candy and cookies only to find lots of Baggies each containing something partially eaten—a graham cracker, cookie, breakfast bar, candy bar. It would take Becky days to consume these foods because she would eat them one bite at a time. Sometimes the food sat in Baggies so long that it became stale and I'd throw it out, which made her angry. You could see the same thing in the refrigerator and freezer. And although she never talked about dieting, some days she hardly ate anything, while other days I wondered where all the food went.

One day after returning from dropping her off at a lacrosse game, I was greeted at the door by the concerned faces of my other two children.

"Is Becky okay?" they asked.

"Yes," I responded. "Why?"

"Because she threw up right after she ate," they replied in unison. "We flushed the toilet."

In that moment, I knew in my heart that Becky was bulimic. I didn't know how long it had been going on, but somehow I knew it was true. And as much as we'd prayed in our group that hidden things would be revealed, it broke my heart to discover this.

Normally, we respect our children's privacy, but in this case I knew I needed to search her room for clues. There I found a food diary in which she recorded every single thing she ate each day along with the calories. Some days she consumed hardly anything. On the days when she ate what she perceived to be a lot of food, she wrote degrading comments about herself in bold letters: FAT, UGLY, and AWFUL. It broke my heart to read these words. I sunk to the carpet with that food diary in my lap, and a floodgate of tears opened up. I couldn't stop crying.

YOU CAN'T MAKE ME!

The next few months were hard. My husband was sympathetic to my concerns, but only to a point. And even though we took our daughter to see a counselor specializing in eating disorders, my husband was not as convinced as I that she truly had a problem.

"Maybe this is just the beginning. Maybe we've caught it before it becomes a big problem," he told me. "After all, Becky denied there was anything wrong."

I wanted to believe him, but the psychologist suspected the worst, and so did I. She also explained that unless Becky admitted to having a problem, she couldn't work with her on an outpatient basis. She recommended we go to a center for eating disorders for in-depth testing and advice. I made the appointment and took my daughter, but she denied everything and answered all the questions the way she thought they were supposed to be answered.

Based on her past behaviors, however, the staff at the center agreed that I had reason to be concerned. Since they didn't have an opening for Becky in their program, they recommended we find a psychologist she'd feel comfortable with and suggested that Becky continue to meet with the nutritionist.

Amid her sobs on the way home, Becky cried, "I'm not going to talk to any strangers! You can't make me, Mom! You can waste your money if you want to, but I am *not* going to cooperate."

A TEMPORARY REPRIEVE

In the midst of this situation, I was preparing to lead a summer missions trip to Costa Rica. This would be the third trip Becky and I had gone on together, but this time I was co-leader of the trip. We left two weeks after our appointment at the eating disorder center and had a wonderful time together. When we came back, I got sick with influenza. Soon afterward, Becky came down with mono. During our illnesses, the eating disorder issue was temporarily forgotten.

In the middle of August, Becky started her sophomore year slightly heavier than she had ended her freshman year. The moment school began, she restricted her eating and lost 20 pounds in five weeks. I knew what was happening, and it broke my heart. At 5 feet she weighed 110 pounds, which isn't off the charts. That's the difficult thing: Bulimia is not as easy to recognize as anorexia because your child still eats. Also, as in my daughter's case, many kids who are bulimic also exhibit signs of anorexia by restricting their food intake. When they can't take it anymore, they binge and purge. As much as I tried, Becky refused to talk with me about the issue. My husband was now as concerned as I. Yet we didn't know what to do. So far, our efforts had seemed futile, and when we met with the psychologist, she reminded us again that outpatient therapy with her would work *only* with Becky's cooperation.

Finally, early on a cloudy September morning, the mother of Becky's best friend showed up at my doorstep. Susan apologized for the intrusion and asked if we could talk. Instinctively, I knew what it was about and welcomed her in. After looking down and clearing her throat a few times she said, "Becky told my daughter that she is bulimic and has been for almost three years. I hate to interfere, but I just thought you ought to know." Although Susan and I had never spent time together before, I felt comfortable talking with her and told her what we'd done so far about our concerns for Becky. Before she left I said, "Susan, I'm so thankful you came and told me. Now we finally have undeniable proof. I know it took a lot of courage. Thank you so much for coming."

After she drove off, I went inside, shut the door to my room and felt a crushing burden and anxiety for my daughter. But in the midst of my tears, I thought, *Now we have the proof we need. We can confront her with the truth and intervene.*

My Moms In Touch group had been aware of my concerns the previous spring, but we'd been off for the summer. Now that we were meeting again, I knew I could trust them with all of my heartache and fears for our daughter. I don't remember everything that happened that morning, but I know that as I opened up about Becky's bulimia, these women felt my pain deeply, and we spent most of the time praying just for her.

This was the beginning of a long and difficult year. I believe that nothing is too hard for God, but I also know He won't force His will on us—nor on a daughter who has no willingness to change. At that time, Becky's mind was too disordered to see clearly the severity of the problem. In her confusion, she couldn't distinguish between lies and truth. Besides, as she told me later on in her recovery process, she had turned her back on God. Although as a young girl she had asked Jesus to forgive her sins and trusted Him for her eternal security, she wasn't ready yet to believe He had good plans for her life. She wouldn't trust Him enough to allow Him to change her mind and will, to accept that she was created as His special child. She pushed away all the comfort and love a relationship with God has to offer.

PROBLEMS MULTIPLY

We began to realize that over the past year and a half, darkness had set up a beachhead in Becky's life in several ways. In addition to the bulimic bingeing and purging, she had started cutting herself to numb her emotional pain. She not only listened to dark, violent music, but she also wasted far too much time in the world of MySpace and Facebook. It was only in the days to come that my husband and I would realize how subtly these things had crept in and taken over her life.

Our Moms In Touch circle continued to pray for wisdom in the days ahead—that God would lead us to the right people who could help Becky and work out the times for all the appointments. We prayed for protection for Becky and that she would turn from darkness to God's light. And finally, we prayed that God might use this experience for Becky's good and for His glory. In the tough days to come, these dear moms would shed tears, pray, and stand with me when I needed it most.

God answered the prayers for direction immediately. We went back to the psychologist we'd met in the spring. A wise and caring Christian woman, she had experience in helping patients with eating disorders or who cut themselves. Since Becky could no longer deny the eating disorder, the psychologist agreed to build an individualized outpatient program as long as Becky agreed to certain accountabilities. This psychologist directed Becky's recovery program and became the base of a pyramid of professionals who would help her through this process.

Yet since Becky was in outpatient treatment, my husband and I, in essence, became the ones who had to hold her accountable just like staff in an inpatient facility. The psychologist warned us that things might get worse before they got better. And did they ever!

THE CRISIS DEEPENS

Becky was seeing a nutritionist and a medical doctor. She was eating balanced meals and staying out of the bathroom after eating. She was allowing me to check for cuts, but it was obvious she wasn't embracing recovery. Just as in early childhood, Becky acted like a young mustang, butting against the edges of the corral for more freedom. As I met with Becky's counselor weekly to discuss her progress and receive guidance on how we could better parent her through this time, the psychologist helped me realize that in our effort to find balance between giving her clear rules and allowing her choices, my husband and I had let the reins fall too loosely in a few key areas. We had trusted Becky completely and had not monitored what music she was purchasing, what she was doing on the computer, or even what time she went to bed.

As the weeks went on, the psychologist sensed that something was holding Becky's progress back. As she and I met and talked, it became apparent to her that the violent music, as well as lack of boundaries on computer use and bedtime, was hindering her progress. She recommended we see a family therapist and work out a contract with Becky regarding these key issues. I went home and decided to start with the simplest one: bedtime. I told Becky to start unwinding by 10:00 or 10:30 in her room (which has never had a computer or TV in it) on school nights, and lights were to be out by 11:00. By the third night when she realized this schedule wasn't going to be a passing phase, she got upset and stormed off to her room where she battled the temptation to cut. Unbeknownst to my husband and me, she had broken a blade off the razor that she used to shave her legs and kept it in her nightstand drawer.

As her mind argued back and forth, she started to put the razor down, but at the last minute she impulsively cut herself instead. For the first time, Becky cut so deeply we had to rush her to the emergency room (ER) where they glued the cut together. As we drove to the hospital Becky kept saying over and over, "I'm so sorry" and "I can't believe it's come to this."

Rather than crying, she just seemed to be numb and surprised by it all. Since we told the doctors that she was in therapy for an eating disorder, they let her come home with us. She spent the night with me while my husband slept in her room. The next morning we went to see the psychologist to process what had happened and regroup.

This was the beginning of a two-month struggle as we added family therapy appointments to draw up a contract for monitoring bedtime, computer usage, music, and friendships. It was the toughest part of her recovery, but it was necessary to remove the obstacles. It wasn't until we bought some sophisticated monitoring software that we realized the enormous amount of time she had been spending on the computer and what she was doing. For a period of time, we had to block Facebook and MySpace completely.

Finally, by spring our lives had calmed down and we were able to see a lot of progress. I wrote Becky a letter telling her how much I loved her and that although I wouldn't have chosen to have all of this happen, I could already see many good things coming out of it—another answer to prayer.

I was thankful she was doing better but knew she still struggled with her body image and her desire to lose weight. And even though she'd kept herself from purging and cutting ever since the ER visit months before, she hadn't completely given up her eating disorder. "Mom, it's an option to fall back on," she told me one day, "but, someday, I really want to share my story to help other girls."

After a busy school year, during which Becky managed to squeeze in every appointment without missing many classes, summer arrived. Becky had been in treatment for nine months, and in June she decided to go on a Christian retreat. When she returned, she was on fire for God. She'd had a breakthrough that washed a lot of her disappointment away. In fourth grade, when her body started to change, she began to think God hadn't created her the way *she thought* He should. That disappointment led to distrust and disbelief that His ways are right and good. However, through the messages given during the retreat, the Christian music, and a powerful skit that depicted some of the very things she had struggled with (bulimia and cutting), she felt God's love for her and realized how trustworthy He is. She also realized that He wants good things for her—not necessarily easy and painless things, but good things. Most important, it sunk in that the Lord Jesus was right there with her in the midst of her darkest times. The "soil" of her heart had been tilled the previous nine months, and she was finally ready to plant the seeds of renewal and connect with God. After she shared her experience of self-hatred and rebellion with the retreat leaders, they prayed with her and encouraged her to share her story with peers.

Since that weekend, Becky has told her story to two groups at school and at church. While she doesn't go into all the details, her message is simple yet powerful: "I didn't trust God. I thought He'd made a mistake in how He created me, so I turned my back on Him. I entered a dark world of destruction until my secret was exposed. And though other paths may seem right, they are really lies that lead you into more and more darkness."

Each time she spoke, she thanked God for her friend who had the courage to inform an adult. She also thanked the people who influenced her and worked with her during her recovery process.

Although I can rejoice now, I didn't know how this story would turn out. I struggled with two things during this tumultuous time: fear and loneliness. My biggest fear was that my daughter wouldn't get better. At times, in my frustration and impatience with her slow progress, I tried to take charge of her spiritual life. It was then that Becky clearly told me that this was *her* spiritual life and that I couldn't live it for her. She was right. I had to release her to God no matter the outcome. This was terribly hard and there were points along the way when all I could do was groan out in my pain and ask God to take away my fears and heal my heartache. Yet time after time as I did, I discovered that He was sufficient.

One of the verses that I clung to during this painful period was Jeremiah

29:11: " 'For I know the plans I have for you,' declares the Lord, 'plans to prosper you and not to harm you, plans to give you hope and a future.' "

I clung to the words *hope* and *future*. And when fear and worry began to cloud my mind, I remembered what God had done for us in the past. I recalled who He is and always has been. I took my focus off my circumstances and redirected it to Him who is my hope and future. Then I would pray the same verse for Becky, asking that she would believe that God has plans for her—good plans, not necessarily easy ones, but plans to give her a bright future and hope.

It was a long process that is not over yet, but I'm so grateful for the moms who continue to pray for my daughter. Looking back, I can see God's fingerprints all along the way. I know that Becky still struggles with her self-image. Yet she now has the tools to help herself. She learned the hard way that secrets are what keep us in bondage and darkness. She knows that it's okay to fail and make mistakes because God can bring good out of bad. No matter what, she knows the Almighty God who can redeem anything. And in the process, I've learned to trust the One who loves my daughter even more than I do.

Pray Together

"For I know the plans I have for you," declares the Lord, "plans to prosper you and not to harm you, plans to give you hope and a future."

—Jeremiah 29:11

God,

You are my hope. I pray the precious child that You have entrusted to me will believe that You have good plans for her and a bright future. Lord, I pray for my dear sister in Christ whose son or daughter is caught in a web of deception and darkness. Wipe away her tears and give her Your peace as she finds her hope in You and perseveres with other moms in prayer. In Your holy name, amen.

This is the confidence which we have before Him, that, if we ask anything according to His will, He hears us. And if we know that He hears us in whatever we ask, we know that we have the requests which we have asked from Him.

—1 JOHN 5:14–15 (NASB)

————

Prayer is the conduit through which power from heaven is brought to earth.

—DR. OLE HALLESBY, *Prayer*

Chapter Five
An Infant's Struggle for Life
by Cheri Fuller of Oklahoma

Arms loaded with gifts and bright balloons, we huddled around the door of the birthing suite at Lakeside Renaissance Center in Oklahoma City waiting to hear our grandbaby's first cry. The four grandparents plus several aunts and uncles chatted, paced, prayed, and waited. Excitement was in the air. As the group grew to include friends, so did my anticipation to see my son Justin's first baby. This would be the first grandchild on both sides of the family. And though my stomach growled in hunger, I wasn't about to go buy a sandwich at the cafeteria and miss Baby Caitlin's arrival!

Tiffany, Justin's wife, had gone into labor several times in the last weeks, but the doctor was able to stop the contractions, which gave the baby more time to safely develop in the womb. This time the process would not be stopped. We hoped for a healthy baby and that everything would go smoothly for Tiffany.

After a few hours, the door opened and a nurse stuck her head out. "Where are the grandma and grandpa?" she asked. Noting the four of us, she said, "Delivery is getting closer. You're going to get to see your grandbaby soon."

BREATHTAKING NEWS

As "soon" wore on, we realized something might be wrong. Doctors and nurses raced in and out of the delivery room with worried expressions. Anxiety replaced the excitement I'd felt only moments before.

A short while later a staff member told us that Caitlin was in severe respiratory distress—she couldn't breathe. Her lungs weren't developed enough to function on their own, and the umbilical cord had wrapped around her neck, causing fluid to fill her lungs. Instead of being allowed to cuddle our granddaughter, suddenly we were riding in a car following an ambulance that was rushing Caitlin and her parents to the best neonatal intensive care unit (NICU) in the region.

FINDING HOPE IN THE NICU

A heavy weight of anxiety and sadness hung over family and friends huddled in the NICU waiting room. Instead of snapping photos, we were offering silent prayers, pleading with God for our sweet grandbaby's life, and worrying through the night and early morning hours. We ached with compassion, empathizing with what Justin and Tiffany were going through. They were separated from their first child, sequestered in the waiting room with us. Strain, fatigue, and fear marked their faces. Poor Tiffany barely got to recover from labor.

From the beginning, the doctors called Baby Caitlin "a fighter" and her courageous spirit struggled for life as the medical team labored. Even with a ventilator, a high-powered oscillator, blood transfusions, and medication, Caitlin's survival was tenuous. All we heard from the medical staff for 48 hours was, "Still critical . . . the next few days will tell . . . wait and see."

But oh, how grateful we were for Dr. Co, the head NICU physician who kept saying, "Hang in there, Dad," with a compassionate pat on the shoulder to Justin, and a reassuring "Keep praying . . . be patient, Grandmas," to Pat and me.

Yet as the hours dragged on, we were also aware we weren't the only families with a burden. Other parents and grandparents of critically ill infants sat around the room as well, speaking in hushed voices of the latest update on their babies' condition.

On Caitlin's second day in NICU, the doctor allowed immediate family into the cubicle to visit her. Even though we couldn't hold her, we could talk, pray, or sing to her. As my husband and I walked in the first time, I almost reeled at the sight of her tiny body in the sterile isolette. She had an intravenous tube in her leg, a heart monitor taped to her chest, and electrodes attached to her temples, sending messages to monitors that crowded the room. Beeping noises pulsated around us. Her little mouth was covered with a ventilator mask, which was taped on securely. A much-too-large diaper covered her small bottom.

Despite the machines and isolation, the nurses were providing our grandbaby with intimate, loving care. One nurse had attached a little red bow to her dark brown hair in honor of upcoming Valentine's Day. As the caring NICU nurses came in and out, checking her oxygen levels and vital signs, I quietly sang to Caitlin, "Jesus loves you, this we know, for the Bible tells us so." Suddenly I looked up and saw the sign our daughter Ali had made and the staff had taped beside the cubicle:

CAITLIN
For I know the plans that I have for you,
plans to prosper you, plans for peace, plans for hope,
declares the Lord. —[adapted from] Jeremiah 29:11

Hope began to fill my heart and lift my spirit. Those moments with our granddaughter passed too quickly, and then a nurse escorted us back to the waiting room to do just what the doctors had told us: *wait*. As the hours passed, however, instead of just waiting or offering our individual prayers, every family member and friend present got on his or her knees together and fervently prayed for Caitlin and her parents.

AN INTENSIVE CARE UNIT OF PRAYER: BRINGING IN THE REINFORCEMENTS

As we were praying, I was reminded of two critically ill children I'd heard of whose recovery even physicians attributed to a large network of prayer on their behalf. I had interviewed the mothers for my book *When Mothers Pray* and heard their personal accounts of the power released in their children's lives when many, many people gathered to pray for them, both near and far away.

In that moment, I sensed God's quiet whispers saying that just as Caitlin was in a medical intensive care unit, she needed a more intensive level of intercessory prayer. Family and close friends had been praying, but we needed to bring in the reinforcements. I decided that morning to call many others to join us in prayer for her. First I phoned Peggy Stewart, who is my longtime prayer partner, and then I called Flo Perkins, my 75-year-old intercessor and dear friend. The next person I called was Anita, our College and Career Moms In Touch group co-leader, who spread the word among the 15 mothers who weekly gathered at my house. They all began to pray for Baby Caitlin.

In addition, I contacted prayer chains and my Moms In Touch
International friends at the headquarters in California. Family members rallied
their friends and churches to intercede. Soon a huge prayer team stretched
from Oklahoma to Florida, Colorado to California, and around the globe even
to the Black Forest Academy, a missionary kids' school in Germany, and the
Children's Prayer Network of Australia and New Zealand. The large prayer
circle that was amassed included a devoted group of nuns in a western state
and ministries in New York and North Dakota—all who joined their voices in
bringing our granddaughter to God.

Little voices and grown-up ones; short, childlike prayers and mature
ones—God heard Caitlin's name *over and over*, day after day. When doctors saw a
negative change and warned, "This isn't going well; this is what needs to happen
in her lungs," we spread the word through group e-mails and phone calls.

Praying Specifically

Twice a day a mother from our Moms In Touch group (who happened to be a
pediatric specialist) relayed the news of what needed to happen in Caitlin's little
body and lungs. Kay had the marvelous ability to take technical medical reports
from the doctors and turn them into specific, practical prayer requests.

For example, when Caitlin was taking 80 to 100 breaths per minute and
the doctor said that number was too high, Kay passed the word to pray for
her respiration to drop to between 40 and 60 breaths per minute. When her
breathing slowed down, we specifically thanked God for that. And twice in those
weeks several faithful MITI moms came to the hospital and we had an impromptu
prayer meeting right in the waiting area.

As we waited for Caitlin's condition to improve, our family also had the
privilege of praying for the other 23 babies in the NICU at that time, and for
peace and comfort for their worried parents and grandparents. As several of the
infants rallied and went home, we were happy for their families even as we kept
asking God for Caitlin's much-needed turnaround. We asked for more prayer for
the nighttime hours because that was when she suffered setbacks.

The Turnaround

Finally, at the end of the second week, our Caitlin began to turn the corner. In
fact, her doctor told us her X-rays on Friday morning reflected a *different set of
lungs* than the ones from Thursday. Prayers continued as Caitlin was transferred

from the ventilator to an oxygen "space helmet" and began the difficult task of breathing on her own. After another full week of treatment in the neonatal care unit, her lungs recovered enough for our precious granddaughter to go home.

Although Caitlin was in the hospital several times her first few years, she's now an active, bright 11-year-old who loves riding her bike, reading novels, playing tennis, and swimming. She has run with her mom in a 5K race and is on a competitive rock climbing team. Whatever Caitlin does, she pursues it with energy and enthusiasm. She still has asthma, but has overcome each obstacle she's faced—and she loves life, her family, friends, and Jesus with exuberance and joy.

One Saturday recently, my heart skipped a beat as we watched Caitlin climb 90 feet straight up in a competitive rock climbing competition and receive an award. Our little "fighter" (as the NICU doctors called her) has a determination and focus that are stunning to watch, and yet a sensitivity to the hurts and needs of others. Recently, she qualified as one of only 37 young people in America to compete in the USA Nationals in rock climbing in Boulder, Colorado. How thankful we are for our granddaughter's life, and what a blessing she is to us all.

We are also well aware that not every situation in which a family unites in prayer ends in a positive outcome as Caitlin's did. Having lost a baby in a premature delivery, I know the pain of losing a child, and it's one of the deepest sorrows one has to bear in this life.

But through this medical crisis, we learned so much about the importance of covering our grandkids in prayer and giving God specific requests. We also were struck by the power of praying for them not just by ourselves, but *together with others*, creating a network of love and intercession. Sometimes we all need to bring in reinforcements for whatever needs or battles our children and grandchildren face.

Perhaps your grandchild isn't in a medical crisis like our granddaughter was, but has another type of challenge: a learning or behavior problem, a broken family as a result of divorce, or an individual struggle. He or she may wrestle with addiction or go down the wrong path that ends in legal consequences. In whatever we or our children and grandchildren face, I've discovered prayer is just inviting God into our needs. And for all grandparents, not only our grandkids' infancy, but also throughout their lives, there is never a time they don't need our prayers.

Pray Together

Pray in the Spirit on all occasions with all kinds of prayers and requests. With this in mind, be alert and always keep on praying for all the saints.

—Ephesians 6:18

———————

Again I tell you that if two of you on earth agree about anything you ask for, it will be done for you by my Father in heaven. For where two or three come together in my name, there am I with them.

—Matthew 18:19-20

———————

Thank You, God, for Your promise that when two or more grandmothers or moms gather in prayer for our precious ones, You will be right there with us. I pray for the grandma who is in the "waiting room" right now, greatly anxious about her grandchild's condition or problems. Please comfort her and wrap her mind and heart with peace. Bring healing to her grandchild's entire body, soul, and spirit. In Your precious name, amen.

Let this be written for a future generation,
that a people not yet created may praise the Lord.

—PSALM 102:18

It is in prayer and its answer that the interchange of love between the Father and His child takes place.

—ANDREW MURRAY, *With Christ in the School of Prayer*

CHAPTER SIX
CALMING THE "STRONG WILLED" STORM
by Cindy Foster of South Carolina

FOR THE FIRST TIME IN HER LIFE, MY DAUGHTER BETHANY IS MESMERIZED BY SOMEONE OTHER THAN HERSELF—HER DAUGHTER, LEIGHTON. TEN YEARS AGO, WHEN BETHANY WAS 13, THE IDEA OF HER BEING HAPPILY MARRIED WITH A DELIGHTFUL LITTLE BABY GIRL WOULD NEVER HAVE ENTERED MY MIND. THERE WERE TIMES BACK THEN WHEN I DIDN'T EVEN EXPECT TO KNOW WHERE BETHANY WOULD BE WHEN SHE WAS AN ADULT, MUCH LESS BE PART OF HER LIFE.

The day Bethany entered our world and captured our hearts, she already had a keen sense of self and a strong personality. At first, her precious little face and precocious mind were adorable. But when she became a toddler, her newly realized independence made everyday life a battle. It was evident, even at that early age, that a storm was brewing. Bedtime, teeth brushing, hair combing, what to wear, and eating were all optional and a source of negotiation, at least in her mind. Before she was two she was speaking in full paragraphs and could clearly articulate what she wanted and how she felt about it.

As social as she was, I thought Bethany would love school, but it just added more rules to her life and more opportunities for her to buck the system. Homework was a nightmare. What should have been a simple routine, especially for someone as smart as she was, became a source of conflict. Some mornings I was so exhausted over the battle just to get her dressed and fed and off to school that I would burst into tears. Was motherhood supposed to be this hard? Was I doing something wrong? Why couldn't anything with Bethany be easy? Would our mother-daughter relationship always be this strained and frustrating?

I was nervous about our future. We were in a boat on a rough sea and the waves were getting bigger.

A CHANGE OF PERSPECTIVE

God knew I could not persevere alone and brought Moms In Touch into my life. Up until then my prayers were anemic at best. I did not pray outside of church and never thought to pray *about something* let alone *with someone*. But prayer was what I desperately needed. At a retreat in Charlotte, North Carolina, I heard Fern Nichols speak about prayer actually being a legacy. I was caught up in that vision. I could be the praying mom and someday the praying grandmother she talked about. My children, their children, and their grandchildren would know that I prayed for them. Even though my mother had not left me this legacy, I could start the chain! What an awesome privilege.

I dove wholeheartedly into Moms In Touch and became a leader for my group. As I prepared each week by reading the Bible, I came to know who God is and to know more about the relationship between us. I started having regular prayer times, during which I would pray and read the Scriptures. This became my lifeline, giving me peace in the middle of our tumultuous storm. As a mom, carving out time alone was a little tricky. I discovered that if I sat in my car in the driveway with the doors locked, I could actually find some solace. Soon my children learned that was "Mommy's quiet time," and they would take their requests to Daddy or wait until I came back inside.

I clung to my prayer time and my Moms In Touch meetings as Bethany entered her preteen years. Bethany wanted adultlike freedom at an early age—freedom to stay up late, to go to parties, to make all her own decisions. She was fearless, but naïve and immature at the same time. She struggled with authority, especially mine. Why did I have so many rules? Why didn't I let her do what she wanted?

By middle school she thought she was ready for boy-girl parties. At 12 she declared that, since it was only a year until her next birthday, she should be allowed to go to PG-13 movies.

She should have been a lawyer. Every time we fought, she could make a stronger case than I could. And she certainly wouldn't accept my reasoning without at least slamming a door in my face or shoving an "I hate you" into my heart.

But I knew I could not let go, give in, or give up.

My MITI moms sat beside me for those many years. They prayed with me, and often *for* me, when I didn't have the emotional stamina to pray. And God slowly changed me from a desperate, hopeless mom, to a praying, hopeful, trusting mom.

Every time the winds rocked the boat, which was often, I ran to the God I had come to know. I learned all the names and attributes of God in the Bible, many of which have Hebrew origins. I clung to *Jehovah Jireh*, the God who provided for me in my time of great need. I cried out to *Jehovah Shalom*, who gave me His peace that is not from this world. I called upon *Jehovah Sabbaoth*, the Commander in Chief, who deployed His heavenly hosts to battle the attacks of the enemy on my family. Jesus also has special names. He was my Rock and my Redeemer. He could move mountains and perform miracles. God's Holy Spirit was my Counselor and my Comforter.

THE STORM RAGES

I think of storms as ebbing and flowing, but with Bethany in the house there was no calm. As she went into her teen years, things went from bad to worse to "I don't know how I am going to survive." She lied to my husband and me. She manipulated us. She pitted us against each other. I was concerned about the example she was setting for our other children and was heartbroken over the turmoil that surrounded her. Yet I loved her with all my heart.

Our youngest child was born when Bethany was 14. With two young children and two teenagers, I was physically and emotionally exhausted every single day. Most of my energy went into staying on top of Bethany's behavior and schoolwork. She was not performing anywhere near her potential and took advantage of my exhaustion and the necessary attention I had to give to our little ones. Our marriage was buckling under the strain.

Bethany was a tall, beautiful blonde, but still a young teenager and growing up too fast. She partied too much and placed too much value on her outward appearance. Her looks seemed to be all that mattered to her. I must admit, she had style—no piercings, Goth, or tattoos for her, just the latest in designer fashions. But the clothes she chose made her look older than she was. The neckline cut became too low, the style too flirty and provocative for her age. She began wearing more makeup and getting attention from older boys who probably had no idea how young she was.

She chose friends who had little accountability, and she balked when we gave her boundaries. One of my frequent prayers for her was that she would get caught—and she did. She would often say, "Everyone else does it, but I am always the only one who gets caught!" She saw it as a great injustice. I believe it was God's protection.

One of the lowest points of my mothering came when Bethany was 15 and our youngest child was still a baby. One morning, before dawn, I was awakened out of my sleep. There was no reason for it, no noise in the house, no bad dream. I remember thinking, *Why did I just wake up?* As I lay in bed, I heard our front door open. I knew it was Bethany coming in. I went downstairs and confronted her. She denied that she had been out and said she had come downstairs because she didn't feel well. In my heart I knew she was lying. My husband joined us, but he believed Bethany and defended her. I felt alone. Our family was in total chaos, and I felt as if I had nothing left in me to give.

My lifeline was Moms In Touch International. Through the love and prayers of my sweet MITI friends, I felt heard, understood, and supported. Later it was confirmed that Bethany had, in fact, been leaving our home after we went to bed to hang out with an older boy. I believe God allowed me to wake up that morning specifically to catch her in the act. It was clearly an answer to prayer.

Off to College

After four tumultuous years of high school in two schools and a stint at boarding school thrown in, we saw some victories. First, Bethany was actually accepted into college. Second, and more important, though her lifestyle and choices were disheartening, little by little God had totally restored our relationship. He had given me a new love and hope for her, and she received it. We continued to be close, despite the trials, and I continued to pray for her with all my energy.

Sending Bethany away to college was a real milestone. As we drove up to the hotel for her orientation, I realized it was the same hotel I'd stayed in eight years earlier when I'd heard Fern talk about the legacy of prayer. That weekend I had prayed my heart out for Bethany, and now she was moving to this same city to go to college. When I got home, I started my first college and career MITI group.

"Calm waters" didn't flow into our life with Bethany often, but for a few years things seemed manageable. The strong storms came once again when

Bethany was not "invited back" to school after three years due to poor grades. I continued praying in MITI for her as she floundered and drifted in and out of jobs and occasional college classes.

Still balking at rules and accountability, she continued to push the limits. She rotated between coming home and crashing at friends' houses, where she didn't pull her own financial weight. She walked away from debt, not understanding that real consequences existed for over-spenders. When faced with a penalty, she'd ask, "How come nobody told me?" She was equally naïve when she ignored several speeding tickets and her license was suspended.

"You mean I can't drive?" she asked. "I have to! I need to work!"

By this time, the foundation of prayer that I had built upon for many years had become a solid place for me to stand strong. I truly put my hope in God's grace and mercy. I trusted Him with this child He had given me to love and raise.

CHARTING A NEW COURSE

While I was on a retreat one weekend, Bethany called to tell me she was going on a date with a young man named Alex. I was surprised when she went through a checklist of reasons we would like him. She told me her dad would like him because Alex liked Frank Sinatra. Check. Her brother James would like him because he played golf well. Check. And I would like him because his mom was in Moms In Touch. Check!

We met Alex later that month when Bethany brought him home for her 22nd birthday. We were impressed with his good manners and respectful attitude. When I met his mom, we realized we both had been at the same MITI retreat 12 years earlier. Bethany wondered if we had prayed together.

Before I could answer, Alex said, "You did, Mrs. Foster, because you were *all* praying together." He was right. Two Moms In Touch moms, one from New Jersey and one from North Carolina, prayed in a crowd at the same time in what seemed like the most random of circumstances. But nothing is random with God.

Bethany and Alex became serious quickly. Was this Bethany's future husband? I'd been praying for Bethany and her future family for years. Everything was moving forward when another storm hit. Bethany told us she and Alex were expecting a child. They planned to live together; they weren't sure they were ready to commit to marriage before the baby was born.

Alex's mom and I had already been praying together, and we called on God who can move mountains to do "immeasurably more than all we ask or imagine"

(Ephesians 3:20). Within two days Alex called, not knowing our prayer. He said, "Mrs. Foster, I just want to let you know that Bethany and I decided to get married." The mountains were moved. God answers prayer! Sometimes it takes many years and sometimes only hours, but He is faithful.

With only two months of preparation, Bethany and Alexander stood before God on a beautiful spring day and entered a marriage covenant. And then came Baby Leighton, born to two parents who had been prayed for most of their lives.

God has used Leighton's little life to transform Bethany's self-centered focus. Looking back, I can see that Bethany was not a happy child, but she is happy now, happier than I've ever seen her. As passionately as she dove into things we didn't like, she's now passionately and wholeheartedly diving into her new roles as wife and mother. God is answering years of prayers for her maturity, and He's using a little baby girl to do it.

Because God is always faithful, we are now reaping a harvest since Bethany prays for Leighton regularly. This legacy is more than I could have ever asked for or imagined. The storms are over. God stilled the waves. He sustained me, strengthened me, and comforted me. Through prayer, He moves mountains, performs miracles, and creates legacies. Time to start a Grandmothers In Touch!

Pray Together

Now to him who is able to do immeasurably more than all we ask or imagine, according to his power that is at work within us, to him be glory in the church and in Christ Jesus throughout all generations, forever and ever! Amen.

—Ephesians 3:20–21

Heavenly Father,
We praise You because You are kind and merciful. Great is Your faithfulness!
Please sustain the moms of challenging children. Give them strength to set
boundaries and the boldness to persevere in prayer for their children. Surround them
with other praying moms, who can help them pray for their children's protection
and that their children will be caught when doing wrong. Give them Your peace in
the middle of the storm. In Jesus' name, amen.

How gracious he will be when you cry for help! As soon as he hears, he will answer you.

—ISAIAH 30:19

Prayer is the language of a man burdened with a sense of need.
—E. M. BOUNDS, *The Weapon of Prayer*

Chapter Seven
LIFE WITH A DRUG-ADDICTED TEENAGER
by a Virginia mom

ONLY FAMILIES WHO HAVE LIVED WITH AN ADDICT CAN UNDERSTAND HOW ADDICTION TURNS YOUR WHOLE LIFE UPSIDE DOWN. HOW IT MAKES YOU FEEL ALONE, TOO ASHAMED TO SHARE WITH ANYONE ELSE. HOW YOU LOCK UP YOUR WALLET AT ALL TIMES. HOW LIGHTLY YOU SLEEP, KNOWING THAT YOUR LOVED ONE TAKES ADVANTAGE OF YOUR DEEP SLEEP TO GET HIGH. HOW EVERY SIREN MAKES YOU CRINGE IN FEAR UNTIL HE WALKS THROUGH THE DOOR AND YOU HUG HIM ONE MORE TIME. HOW MEAN HE CAN GET WHEN YOU TRY TO PREVENT HIM FROM USING AGAIN. HOW YOU FEAR TO LEAVE THE HOUSE IN CASE HE'LL DO SOMETHING AWFUL WHILE YOU'RE GONE. HOW ACCUSTOMED YOU BECOME TO HAVING SOMEONE ELSE DECIDE THE FATE OF YOUR CHILD.

I didn't want anyone to know that our middle son, the one with a penchant for wearing T-shirts promoting drug-culture music, had been caught using drugs at school for the third time, and that his fate was in the hands of the school administration. I didn't want the Moms In Touch women to know. After all, I had met with them only once and that was when our eldest son was about to graduate from high school—with honors. And I certainly didn't want to breathe a word of our predicament to the parents of my youngest son's preschool friends. I was afraid the nice families wouldn't want their children to play with a boy whose parents had failed to keep one of their sons away from drugs. I know I wouldn't have allowed my kids to play with the children of a family with a drug-addicted child.

When our kids were young and innocent, I thought our great parenting skills would prevent them from doing anything as disdainful as using illegal drugs. But, I had failed that parental report card. I felt alone and ashamed.

SCHOOL HEARINGS

Jonathan had been caught under the influence of drugs at school—twice. After my husband and I endured the humiliating meetings with authorities, Jonathan eventually was allowed to return to school. But the school has strict consequences for repeat offenders. In the opening week of 10th grade, he was caught smoking pot by a police officer, which was Jonathan's third offense. A hearing with the Office of Student Leadership would decide if our son—the boy who used to offer grace before dinner with such beautiful, genuinely heartfelt prayers—would be expelled from the public school system. Forever.

The waiting period was emotionally excruciating. With Jonathan suspended from school for two months, I became a recluse. I didn't trust him enough to leave him alone at home. Before this, I had been able to attend one college Moms In Touch meeting where I had prayed for my eldest son, who was now away at university. But with Jonathan under my constant watch, it would be a long time before I could pray with them again.

Finally the verdict came in the mail: Jonathan could not return to school until he had graduated from a substance-abuse program. Even though my slender son didn't talk to us much, I could tell he felt the gravity of the situation. Jonathan's dream had been to be accepted to college in three years, and he had enrolled in advanced and honors courses to meet that goal. During these two months out of school, I had encouraged him to teach himself these courses, using his textbooks. That motivation dwindled after a few days. But now he was about to miss even more school, and he knew it would be difficult to catch up.

I was grateful that Jonathan desperately wanted to finish 10th grade and not have to repeat it. However, that meant we needed to find a substance-abuse program where he could also attend school. After much searching and consulting, we found a one-year Christian residential drug-abuse program for boys, which also offered Jonathan the opportunity to complete his sophomore year. This facility was an hour's drive away, and we were allowed to visit every other Saturday.

TOO EMBARRASSED TO PRAY ABOUT JONATHAN

When Jonathan entered the residential program, I started praying with the college Moms In Touch group again. But I prayed only for my eldest son because I was too embarrassed to share with the other moms about our struggles with Jonathan. It was a burden I was trying to carry on my own. Eventually, however, the moms in the group started asking the usual questions about kids and family.

Reluctantly, I shared about Jonathan. The women's compassion surprised me. They invited me to pray for Jonathan in our MITI group. Another mom shared that her middle son was also in rehab for drug abuse. Yet she wasn't ashamed to express her emotions or to ask for prayer. God put her in my life as an example of how to deal with this difficult time. Thus began my journey of praying for my children, and my friends' children. I was able to witness God answer prayer after prayer. The answers regarding Jonathan came too, but they came slowly.

Jonathan did well academically and socially at the rehabilitation school, but his heart remained hardened to God's love and forgiveness through Jesus Christ. He still had not become a Christian. And through it all, my Moms In Touch group became my support. Week after week of witnessing answered prayers brought me closer to God than ever before. I studied the Bible more than I ever had.

As God began showing me that I was not the one in control, a heavy burden of shame, grief, and responsibility was lifted off my shoulders. God slowly helped me become brave enough to share with my friends and family about our real struggles. They often asked how I could be so happy despite the difficulties. This gave me the opportunity to share with them my hope that is in God alone.

During this time of concentrated prayer, Jonathan graduated from the residential program in 14 months, and he continued there as a day student to finish 11th grade as well. Since he had fulfilled the requirement of graduating from a substance-abuse program and had done so well in this school, Jonathan was allowed to return to our public school for his senior year.

I began praying in an MITI group that gathered specifically for students at his high school. It gave me hope to know that other MITI moms were supporting me with their prayers and love. And I needed it when I found out that my son had returned to drugs despite two years of residential treatment. By March of his senior year, Jonathan had been suspended three times: once for snorting Vicodin at his desk, once for misusing his computer privileges, and a third time for coming to school under the influence of marijuana. By his third suspension, the school system had lost all patience with his disregard for their rules and the law.

THE FINAL VERDICT

Just a couple of months before his graduation, Jonathan was called before the official school board to defend why they should not expel him forever. Some friends advised us to hire an attorney to defend Jonathan. But we knew our son was guilty as charged, and we decided to let him face the board without counsel. While my heart ached watching him suffer, I knew that Jonathan needed to endure the consequences for his actions. His hearing was set for the same time as my MITI group, and I was encouraged to know the moms were praying for the hearing while it was going on.

I especially needed that encouragement because I felt intimidated. The three school board members and the guidance counselor sat in front of us like judges. My husband, son, and I sat on one side of the room, and the principal, director of the Office of Student Leadership, and a school attorney were on the opposite side of the room. It felt as if we were in a court of law.

As the case against Jonathan was presented, I felt so distant from God. When all of Jonathan's offenses were repeated out loud for everyone to hear, I felt as if Satan were sitting in the front pew laughing at me. As each offense was read, I slumped farther and farther down in my seat. *That's not the whole story!* I wanted to shout. *What about all the good things he has done? Where is God? Has He abandoned me? Has He abandoned Jonathan?*

When it was Jonathan's turn at the podium, I was jolted out of my fog. I was shocked to hear what came out of his mouth. He didn't spout excuses or rationalizations or even fling blame. Instead he told the truth. The whole truth! He admitted he had a drug problem and that he was guilty of all charges. He said he thought he needed to enter another Christian rehab program.

A member of the school board asked him, "Why Christian? Are you a Christian?"

Jonathan looked down at the tiled floor, his wavy, dirty-blond hair falling forward. "Well, I haven't been acting like one since I started using drugs."

Then a second miracle occurred. The guidance counselor spoke up. "I will probably get fired for saying this, but, Jonathan, you need to pray to God! I have a deep faith in God and pray every morning. In fact, I prayed about this case before I came in today." I knew then that God had not abandoned me in that courtroom. I couldn't hold back the tears any longer; that woman had jeopardized her job to tell Jonathan about God, his only hope!

After that, two of the three school board members also shared their faith with Jonathan. Then my husband went up to the podium and shared in front of the entire school board. "I heard a sermon on drinking a year ago," he said. "Because I didn't like the things I did or the things I said after drinking a few beers, I asked God to help me stop drinking, and He did!" My strong husband was moved to tears from his confession. He broke down and cried. I couldn't help myself. I started sobbing. My shoulders were shaking, and I couldn't stop crying. God had made His presence known. Even though I wasn't sure if Jonathan had been expelled or not, I was certain that God was there with me, and that our faithful God is good, all the time! I needed that reminder and the prayers of my group to endure what was to come.

Jonathan was suspended for the remainder of the school year, and he thought he had nothing better to do with his life than to remain on a constant high. His idea about entering rehab faded away. He wasn't ready to commit to the discipline rehab required. He became so addicted to drugs that he would wake up in the middle of the night to get high again. He would climb out the window to smoke pot by himself so he could fall back to sleep. Every three to four hours he searched for a way to get high. My heart ached for him. Watching my son spiral downward was agonizing. He wasn't eating. He was gaunt and disheveled.

My husband and I sought advice from friends and family. They offered many suggestions: Forbid him to see his friends, take him to drug counseling, make him go to youth group, send him back to the Christian rehab, send him to military school, get the justice system involved.

Each of these things had already failed, I realized, because it wasn't Jonathan's idea; neither was it ever his intention to quit. Jonathan had always been our strong-willed child. If he was ever forced to do something against his will, he would plot a way to get around the rules.

TWO MONTHS' NOTICE

After much discussion and prayer, my husband and I came to a difficult decision: Jonathan could no longer live with us after his 18th birthday. We gave him two months' notice so he could find a job and a place to live. But he was so addicted to drugs that the only thing on his mind (when his mind was clear enough to think) was where and when he would get high again. By the time his birthday came, he had burned bridges with all of his friends' parents due to his blatant drug abuse. He had nowhere to go. I prepared his favorite birthday dinner, as always, and after blowing out the candles on his cake, he opened his birthday card. Inside was a coupon his father made for $12,000 for enrollment into another drug abuse residential program.

We told him, "When you are ready to quit drugs, we will pay for it. But we just can't help you at home." It had become too disruptive to our family. He knew this day was coming, but he was upset that he had to take his personal belongings with him. He was hoping he could just leave everything at our house. But that would have opened the door for him to come home each time he needed something. He had to be on his own.

"I love you," I told him.

"I love you, too," he said as he prepared to leave. My heart was breaking, but I had to stand firm.

Having to say good-bye to him that night was gut-wrenching. I went to bed, but I couldn't sleep. For years, I had been waking up in the middle of the night to make sure Jonathan was home. But this time, I couldn't check on him. I didn't even know where he was in this big world. And I didn't know if he was okay or not.

Yet God was good throughout the ordeal. We discovered that Jonathan was living under a huge bush at the church behind our house. Every morning before work, my husband would sneak over and check on him, then silently pray over him as he slept, wishing he could kiss his forehead as he had every morning when he was home.

I would wait for his phone call: "Jonathan's fine." And I would heave a sigh of relief. I clung to my Monday morning prayer times with my Moms In Touch group. I knew that everything that was said and prayed about during that hour was held in the strictest confidence. That allowed me to be vulnerable and honest in my prayers.

I begged God to protect Jonathan while he was homeless, to prepare his heart to ask for help, to show us specifically which rehab program we should send him to when he was ready, and, most important, that Jonathan would turn his life over to the Lord Jesus.

SEARCHING FOR THE RIGHT TREATMENT, JUST IN CASE

Over the next three weeks, I spent hours online and on the telephone looking for the best place to send Jonathan and preparing enrollment paperwork. I wanted to be prepared if he ever came to collect his birthday present. I had a Missouri treatment center picked out with a backup program in New York.

Three weeks after Jonathan's birthday, my MITI group met for our last prayer time before school let out for summer. It was awkward to say good-bye not knowing when or if Jonathan would ever come home. We always split into groups of two or three to pray for each other's children. But on this day, the group wanted to pray together for Jonathan. I was so touched that every mom in that room was moved to pray for him. One mom was specific in her prayers. "Make Your presence known to Jonathan *today* in some way, so that Jonathan will draw closer to You *today*." She repeated "today" several times in her prayer.

Jonathan came home that day at 5:30 P.M. He was bone thin and disheveled; his long hair was matted and greasy. It took my breath away seeing him standing on our doorstep, clutching his birthday present in his hand. I wanted to fling my arms around him and welcome him in. But I couldn't let down my guard.

I let him speak first. "Mom," he muttered, "would you still consider putting me in a program?" I was so happy. I just hugged him and didn't want to let go! Then I remembered all of our prayers from that morning, especially the prayer asking God to bring Jonathan to Him *today*, and I started crying uncontrollably knowing God's mercy was on me.

My other two sons came in and exclaimed, "Jonathan! Jonathan!" and joined in the group hug. We clung to each other for five minutes with me sobbing the entire time. Afterward, I told the kids about our prayers for Jonathan that morning and how good God is. My heart melted as Jonathan told us, "I love you, Mom. I love you guys."

FOUND: THE RIGHT TREATMENT CENTER

My husband was on his way to Maryland on a business trip, and my in-laws were coming to stay in three days for a visit, but we dropped everything and packed the van. Jonathan and I took off for Missouri that evening. Jonathan was testy at first. He hadn't expected to leave right then, for it all to happen so fast. But God was gracious, and Jonathan started feeling more comfortable about going after I shared about this specific facility, the many people who recommended it, and why I thought this program was better than any of the others.

Jonathan started to relax, and the two of us began enjoying each other's company just like we used to before drugs turned our lives upside down. The trip took more than 22 hours. The conversation could have been strained or sullen.

But it wasn't. We joked and laughed almost the entire time. We rented a global positioning system for the trip, and I put Jonathan in charge of it. It seemed as though every time we needed it, it froze up. Rather than get frustrated, we laughed together and joked about tossing it out the window.

The experience was a faith journey in a very real sense. We were driving toward the highly recommended program in Missouri on faith because I hadn't yet received confirmation that they were ready for him. Just days before Jonathan had come back home, the facility had sent an e-mail to say 14 of their 15 beds were filled, but they had one more spot for him. I hoped that spot was still open, but I didn't know for sure.

The next morning I found out that we didn't have to change our plans. The Missouri ministry was happy to take in Jonathan.

LAST THOUGHTS

We recently received a letter from Jonathan that read, "It has been 80 days since I have been off drugs, and it feels so good!" When I saw him at Christmas, he had filled out nicely. His hair was cut short, and he shaved every morning. My son was becoming a man.

I believe that prayer is one of God's greatest gifts to us. It is only through prayer that we see our questions answered! If we do not pray, then we miss His glory in our everyday lives. I am grateful to Moms In Touch International for encouraging me to make prayer a routine in my life. When the time comes for Jonathan to leave the program, I know he might have a difficult time transitioning back into a drug-free, productive life. But I have seen God's faithfulness in the past, and I cling to that as I look toward the future.

Pray Together

And we know that in all things God works for the good of those who love him, who have been called according to his purpose.

—Romans 8:28

Heavenly Father,
Forgive us when we doubt Your plan for us and our children. Forgive our impatience while we wait for Your answers. Help us to trust You and Your timing, understanding how deep is Your love for each one of us. Thank You especially for listening to every word spoken to You in prayer, and for Your blessed Scriptures that give us assurance of our hope in You.
It is in Jesus' precious name we pray, amen.

Yet he did not waver through unbelief regarding the promise of God, but was strengthened in his faith and gave glory to God, being fully persuaded that God had power to do what he had promised.

—Romans 4:20–21

The degree to which I know and believe in God's character is the degree to which I can and will trust Him and consequently obey Him.

—attributed to Kay Arthur

Chapter Eight
Pornography Grips a Young Man's Heart
by a Michigan mom

I OPENED THE COMPUTER ROOM DOOR QUIETLY, NOT SURE WHAT I'D SEE. AND THERE WAS MY SON, LOOKING AT INTERNET PORNOGRAPHY. IN A SPLIT SECOND, MY HEART BEGAN RACING, TEARS FILLED MY EYES, AND I FELT LIKE SCREAMING. I COULDN'T BELIEVE WHAT WAS RIGHT IN FRONT OF MY EYES AND IN MY HOME. HOW COULD MY GOOD KID GET CAUGHT UP IN THIS HORRIBLE THING?

I was shocked. Josh had been so great about obeying our computer rules. My husband and I had a terrific relationship with him, and we had every reason to trust him. Yet that night I saw the closed door, which violated our household rule for the computer room, and I felt an inner nudge to go check on him. When I caught him doing something so destructive, anger rose up in me. As disappointed as I was in Josh, my anger wasn't directed at him. Pornography was grabbing at my son, and I didn't want him caught in its dangerous trap.

Years earlier, I had been excited when the doctor told me my third baby was a boy. After two girls, Josh was an extra gift. Over the years, I loved seeing and experiencing the boy-girl differences. They truly are wired differently! Their toys were different, their songs were different, their clothes were different, and their messy rooms were different.

And my prayers were different.

Yes, I prayed for character development and safety for Josh, as I had done

73

for the girls. But safety prayers for Josh were something else entirely. He scared me half to death out on the soccer and lacrosse fields—he played at 100 percent and with every cell in his body. "Heavenly Father, don't let him get hurt" was often the first prayer out of my mouth!

I'd hoped that sports would be the extent of my safety prayers, at least until he began to drive. Then he moved into high school and, simultaneously it seemed, the Internet entered our lives. What began as a mind-enhancing tool soon posed new dangers.

TAKING PROTECTIVE MEASURES

I stepped up my prayers for protection for Josh in high school, particularly when it came to the area of moral purity. I'd heard many stories of innocent boys and girls, some as young as nine, getting hooked into the destructive cycle of Internet porn.

My husband and I took careful steps to mitigate the possibilities of exposure by talking bluntly with Josh, putting a filter on the computer, and telling him the computer room door must be open at all times. We knew that as he grew older, we couldn't follow him around to keep him safe and that the best thing we could do was pray for a strong God-conscience to grow in Josh so he would be able to turn away when he was tempted.

Our weekly high school Moms In Touch group prayed often for our boys to be protected from this vicious moral distraction. We read Psalm 119:37 out loud: "Turn my eyes away from worthless things; preserve my life according to your word," and asked God to keep our children far away from "worthless things." We also prayed that if they were secretly getting involved in Internet pornography, God would intervene and they would be caught.

And caught Josh was! Thankfully, God helped me turn this horrifying moment into a teaching opportunity. We turned off the computer, and, praying a quick prayer for the right words to say, I pulled up a stool beside Josh to talk.

God had already been softening his heart—his blue eyes welled up instantly, and he broke into remorseful sobs. He looked down at the floor and spoke quietly between his tears. "There have been several times that pornography has popped up on my computer," he said remorsefully. "It made me curious. It hasn't been going on long, though. And, Mom, I want you to know that I know it's wrong, and I'm really sorry." I scooted up closer and wrapped my arms around my long, lanky boy.

What we had prayed is exactly what happened: Not only was Josh caught, but I could see in his sobs that his conscience was growing in sensitivity to God. Josh *wanted* to turn away from this temptation, and wasn't that half the battle? Still, I was shaken, and I knew the struggle wasn't over. It's not easy raising boys in a world where pornography is so pervasive and the likelihood of exposure at their friends' homes is so real.

The new awareness of this issue caused us to put a stronger filter on our computers, which included the ability to turn the Internet off at a certain hour when Josh's friends stayed over. At least I knew we could better control it at our house. But when Josh shared with me that some of his friends were beginning to get caught up with Internet pornography too, my heart sank.

It was hard enough to accept the fact that my family was dealing with this issue, but did I really need to talk about it with the other moms? I couldn't get the feeling out of my heart that God wanted me to start the conversation. Thankfully, as awkward as it was to discuss, the moms were open to hear the sad truth. They each determined to add strong filters to their computers and to keep a watchful eye on the boys' computer habits when they were hanging out together. We prayed Psalm 119:37 again for our boys, and also asked God for His wisdom and protection.

THE IMPACT OF A FATHER

My husband became even more intentional about keeping this topic out in the open with our son. He told Josh we wanted to have a "living room chat" with him that evening, which is our family's way of lending seriousness to certain discussions. It usually means someone's in trouble, and our youngest child looked like he really felt the weight of the moment as he quietly walked over to the couch and timidly perched his 6′ 2″ frame on the edge of the cushions.

I clearly remember what my husband told Josh.

"Joshua, do you have any idea what will happen to your heart if you allow your eyes to look at these pictures?" my husband asked. "Do you understand how easily guys get hooked on Internet pornography? Do you realize that your view of women will be skewed forever?"

Then he told Josh that, as his dad, he was going to ask him often about the issue. "Let's talk about it. Let's be accountable."

He then shared with Josh how he keeps his own life protected. He talked about what he and his accountability partner do when they meet every Tuesday morning. I was surprised by his candor, but it turned out to be exactly what Josh needed to hear. My husband described how even grown, happily married men need accountability in this area because of how God created them.

"So every Tuesday morning when I meet with George, we ask each other four key questions: How did you do in your walk with the Lord this week? How did you do as a husband this week? How did you do as a dad this week? And finally, did your eyes see anything that they should not have seen? We are really honest with the answers to these questions, and we then know how to pray for each other specifically. Just knowing I'll be asked these questions every Tuesday morning helps me so much." Then he challenged Josh to do the same with one of his friends.

ON HIS OWN

The high school years flew by, and soon our son and his friends graduated and were ready to spread their wings at college. I struggled with the reality of having to totally let go and trust my son to the Lord, but I also was hopeful that the deterrents we had set up early in his life, the example of his father, and the many prayers for protection and godliness we prayed would affect his daily choices, especially while he was away from home.

I was relieved to find out that the Christian college he was going to had a computer filter system in place. Yet I knew he would have a lot of time off campus as well. I prayed consistently on my own and also with our weekly college Moms In Touch group for God's protection. We prayed that God would continue to help our boys develop a strong sense of truth and godly morals, so that as they went off to college, away from home, they would be able to stand strong in the face of this temptation.

A LESSON LEARNED

As I write this, my son is almost finished with his first year of college, and I am incredibly grateful for the glimpse of God's work in his life that Josh has allowed me to see. Without any prompting, Josh told me that he and Tim, his friend who goes to a school across the country, have decided to hold each other accountable in the area of pornography. They have agreed to call each other if/when either succumbs to the temptation to look at pornography on the Internet, and they've promised to skip their meals for a whole day and take that time to pray for the one who failed. Josh fully understands what pornography will do to his relationships with women and how hard it is to get those images out of his mind.

"Tim and I agreed to fast and pray for each other," Josh said, "because we're trying to follow Jesus' example. He took our failures and loves us even in our weak moments. I want to do that for Tim because that's what Jesus does for me."

What a *huge* answer to years of prayer for Josh—prayers that he'd be caught, that he'd have a repentant heart, and that he'd have the desire to set up an accountability partner. To hear that he has taken this responsibility to guard his heart so seriously brought tears to my eyes and great joy to my heart. I am so relieved that Josh and his dad have done their part. Yet I also know I must never stop praying about this issue for both my son and my husband.

Sometimes I worry that pornography will trap Josh again and then I fear for his future, for his relationships, and that evil will get a foothold in my son's life. But I've found that when I take my fear and anxiety to God, He reminds me that I can trust Him all the time. *All* the time. Whenever I come to the Lord with my concerns, He replaces my fear with hope and peace and joy.

I have learned to never underestimate what God wants to do in my children's lives. I will never give up praying for their hearts and minds! This situation along with others has brought me to the point where I can confidently declare: God is so faithful!

Pray Together

My son, pay attention to what I say;
> listen closely to my words.
Do not let them out of your sight,
> keep them within your heart. . . .
Above all else, guard your heart,
> for it is the wellspring of life.

—PROVERBS 4:20–21, 23

Dear Jesus,
Please encourage the hearts of those mothers who have discovered pornography to be a place of failure in their children's lives. Give them the courage to be faithful in prayer and to know the practical words and actions they should take on their children's behalf. Bring godly influences into their children's lives. Thank You, Lord, that You are so aware of this battle and You are the Victor! In Jesus' name, amen.

Beloved, if our heart does not condemn us, we have confidence before God; and whatever we ask we receive from Him, because we keep His commandments and do the things that are pleasing in His sight. This is His commandment, that we believe in the name of His Son Jesus Christ, and love one another, just as He commanded us.

—1 JOHN 3:21–23 (NASB)

Prayer is how the will of God that is finished in heaven comes into the circumstances of earth. Prayer releases the power of God to accomplish the purposes of God.

—JENNIFER KENNEDY DEAN, *He Leads Me Beside Still Waters*

Chapter Nine
A Divine Heart Transplant
by a Georgia mom

JENNY, SECOND IN A FAMILY OF THREE GIRLS AND THREE BOYS, IS AN UNUSUAL MIX OF ARTISTIC AND GOAL-ORIENTED, ATHLETIC AND "ALL GIRL." AS A YOUNGSTER, SHE HAD LIGHT-BROWN HAIR AND EYEBROWS TOO STRONG AND DARK FOR HER YOUNG FACE. SHE LOVED BOTH BALLET CLASS AND PLAYING KICKBALL IN THE BACKYARD WITH THE FAMILY. I REMEMBER JENNY PLAYING ONE FAMILY GAME OF KICKBALL IN HER PLASTIC DRESS-UP HEELS. AS SHE HEADED FOR FIRST BASE, HER SHOE FLEW OFF. "MY GLASS SLIPPER!" SHE EXCLAIMED. JENNY WAS A DELIGHTFUL LITTLE GIRL, SO EASY TO LIVE WITH SHE ALMOST RAISED HERSELF.

When she was in first grade, I joined a Moms In Touch group. I had no idea how much God would use those weekly prayers for her. Foundational to our group's prayers was that each of our children would experience the miracle of a new spiritual heart. Ezekiel 36:26 describes it like this: "I will give you a new heart and put a new spirit in you; I will remove from you your heart of stone and give you a heart of flesh." During that year Jenny decided to become a Christian. The divine heart transplant! I was grateful.

At the time, I certainly thought her decision to become a Christian was much more significant in her life than my joining a moms' prayer group. But I have since learned that things are not always as they seem.

BIGGER GIRL, BIGGER CHALLENGES

Jenny's middle school years arrived, and now I was an MITI group leader. As Jenny grew bigger, so did the challenges and concerns I brought to prayer each week. Though she was a good student, well-rounded, and happily participating in dance lessons and school clubs, all was not well.

Jenny's longtime best friend abruptly broke off the friendship at the beginning of sixth grade, viciously turning on her. To make matters worse, the friend then took up with a bad crowd that began threatening and harassing Jenny. Since she had never experienced a betrayal of this kind, she was surprised, confused, and devastated by the experience. At Moms In Touch we prayed that Jenny would respond with kindness and find new friends.

Then her former friend began dating an older boy who was already in so much trouble with authorities that he wore a tracking device. His record included a threat to kill his mother. One morning Jenny reported this young man had threatened to beat her up. I was scared. That was the first time that I was forced to really trust God to watch over her. Weekly, my friends at Moms In Touch cried out with me in prayer, asking God to protect her.

That same year I got a glimpse of another side of Jenny besides the sweet daughter we knew her to be. A teacher caught her passing a note that contained vile and disrespectful words. When the teacher called me and read the note over the phone, I was completely shocked and embarrassed. If I had not heard it with my own ears, I would never have believed that Jenny wrote it; I'd never heard her use words like that. Needless to say, my husband and I were supportive of the school's decision to give her detention. Her bad language and disrespectful attitude did not surface again, and our woes seemed to be past tense.

In seventh grade Jenny became a leader of the Christian devotional club at her school. Then we saw our MITI prayers for a new best friend answered beyond what we imagined when Rachel, a Christian, moved to town and was placed in most of Jenny's classes. As eighth graders Jenny and Rachel were coleading the school devotional club. My husband and I were glad to see Jenny putting her leadership skills to positive use.

As Jenny entered ninth grade, she was attending the weekly devotional club at school as well as youth functions at our church. She was a good role model; mothers in our church family wanted their little girls to turn out like Jenny. She was cherished as a loving daughter, sister, and friend. She had become a talented, successful young lady, and those eyebrows of hers turned out to be one of her best features.

We knew our parenting wasn't over, but we assumed Jenny had emerged from the immaturity and poor judgment of her preteen years. We thought the worst was behind us.

By the last half of high school, however, my husband and I sensed a spiritual chill in Jenny's heart. She frequently used her abundance of homework as an excuse to skip youth group; she labeled the kids at the Christian club at school "hypocrites"; she appeared to waver between serving God and serving herself. That she would become wholeheartedly devoted to the Lord Jesus became a theme of our daily prayers for her.

The week before Jenny left for her freshman year of college, we received the dreaded phone call—Jenny had been in an auto accident, and though she was not seriously injured, we needed to get her to the hospital.

She'd made a careless decision that caused a head-on collision, spinning her vehicle across four lanes of heavy traffic. She suffered a fractured cheekbone and a bloody nose, which stained her white shirt, making her injuries look severe.

After I learned about the things that happened and the things that *didn't* happen in the accident, I knew that God was tenderly watching over Jenny. Immediately afterward, three people showed up to help. The first was an off-duty emergency medical technician (EMT) who promptly examined her injuries. Next the familiar face of a high school classmate brought her comfort. And third, a pastor sat down on the curb beside Jenny to pray and read the Bible with her. God provided for her physical, emotional, and spiritual needs right at the scene of the accident.

The next morning in my daily Bible reading, God gave me words to further confirm what I had seen Him do:

The steps of a man are established by the LORD,
> And He delights in his way.

When he falls, he will not be hurled headlong,
> Because the LORD is the One who holds his hand. (PSALM 37:23–24, NASB)

God seemed to have gotten Jenny's attention through the accident. She was bedridden, sore, and grateful for my presence. Before her accident, I could never get her ear. But there she lay, a captive audience now. We talked at length, and I was able to say things I wanted her to hear before she went to college. "Jenny, will you please agree to find some solid Christian fellowship when you get to school?"

"All right, I will."

"You know there will be lots of temptations all around you to neglect your spiritual life."

"Yeah, I know."

Was she really listening? It was difficult to tell . . .

"So you'll do your best to set your priorities and put your relationship with God first?"

"Yeah, I'll try."

Jenny assured me she would seek Christian fellowship and a church in her new college town. But she didn't follow through. She was a conscientious student and somehow was always a little too busy with studies to participate in such activities, an ever-present reminder to me that the Lord Jesus was not first in her life. Though shaken by her brush with death, Jenny's heart toward God remained apathetic and cold.

A MIRACLE HEART TRANSPLANT

By now I had joined a college MITI group, and I continued to pray that Jenny would love God with all her heart, mind, soul, and strength (Luke 10:27).

One week during the summer before her senior year of college, Jenny began calling us daily, telling us about conversations with a fellow student who was helping her "see God." My husband and I were troubled about what kind of god she was suddenly discovering at this secular campus. After a few days, though, she was tearfully speaking of repentance and new faith in Jesus Christ. She told us that for four days she had tried to escape the persistent voice of God but was finally overcome by His irresistible presence and love.

Jenny's sudden, radical encounter with God was as shocking to her as it was turning out to be to us. The God she wanted nothing to do with had invaded her life and ambushed her heart.

A few weeks later she came home and told us more in person. She sat down between her father and me on the couch, and for two solid hours she candidly walked us through her hidden life of rebellion over the past seven years. My husband and I sat paralyzed with shock while Jenny sobbed through her confession.

"I have known for a long time that I wasn't a Christian," she said. "And that I didn't love or want to follow God at all."

"Are you saying that you weren't a true believer, that all this time you were faking it?" her father asked.

"Yes, that's the truth. It was all lies and pretending. I knew if you thought I was saved, I could get away with the stuff I wanted to do."

"But what about when you prayed to receive Christ in first grade?" I asked with a quaver in my voice. "You don't think God saved you then?"

"Well," she answered, "I prayed that prayer many, many times. But nothing like this ever happened, I know that much! I mean, I never experienced a changed heart or a real relationship with Jesus like I have now."

It was slowly dawning on us that this was not just a spiritual high point or recommitment for Jenny. It was God performing a miraculous heart transplant just as He promised, removing her lifeless "heart of stone" and giving her a throbbing "heart of flesh." We began to recognize that all the admirable activities of her childhood—deciding to follow Jesus, leading the Christian club in middle school, teaching five-day Bible clubs, participating in youth mission trips—were not the fruit of a heart for God but were mere activities with no authentic love for Jesus behind them. Jenny's heart had been seeking what God could give her rather than God Himself. But that heart was dead and gone, and now Jenny's new heart was pulsing with love and thankfulness and joy in the Lord God!

Now as Jenny openly confessed the grossest of sins to us, we were stunned and deeply hurt. I experienced moments of feeling betrayed by God. Why hadn't He revealed this awful reality years ago? Why hadn't He answered me when I'd asked that she be caught if she made sinful and harmful choices? The wrongdoings of our other five children had consistently and dramatically been exposed. I also felt shamed as a parent. How could I have missed all of this? How could I have failed so badly in raising her?

It quickly occurred to me that God had graciously hidden the ugliness of Jenny's heart and life until He had dealt with it. In His mercy He had spared us years of anguish, heartache, and strained relationship. Throughout the next month, I found myself thankful and rejoicing but also grieving the loss of the daughter I thought I'd had. Many of my dreams for her were now shattered. During this time, God reminded me that He was the author of Jenny's story. His dreams for her life would come true. How that comforted me!

New Dreams

The first year of Jenny's new life as a Christian was rough. She became romantically involved with the young man who had pointed her to the Lord

Jesus. On the surface it looked great that she was dating a Christian, but this fellow was controlling and unstable. He soon convinced Jenny that she was destined to be his wife. I prayed fervently at home and with friends at Moms In Touch for God's guidance in her life. They broke up, and then Jenny began to truly grow spiritually.

Jenny graduated from college with a solid job and plans to attend graduate school. However, when the business where she was employed closed two weeks later, her plans were disrupted. She was now free to pursue her growing dream of working in overseas missions. Two things were on her heart: impoverished countries and victims of sexual exploitation.

After a few weeks of searching the Internet for various mission agencies and opportunities, Jenny accepted a one-year assignment in an Asian city. While there, God gave her a particular vision and passion to share the gospel with women and girls in that city's brothels. Now He has opened the door for her to return there and join a ministry team with that same purpose. She knows she'll encounter suffering and danger in the red-light districts, but she is prepared for whatever God has for her. She's ready to give her life to help these hurting, hopeless women meet Christ.

God chose to use the prayers of my husband and me and those of my MITI friends in ways far exceeding anything we imagined. He stored up all those prayers for Jenny's wholehearted devotion and is now pouring out His amazing answer!

It's sometimes difficult for me to let go of Jenny for this kind of work. The parents of Jim Elliot found themselves in this position as he prepared to take the gospel of Jesus Christ to the Quichua people in South America. He wrote the following to his parents, referring to Psalm 127:3-5:

> Remember how the Psalmist described children? He said that they were as an heritage from the Lord, and that every man should be happy who had his quiver full of them. And what is a quiver full of but arrows? And what are arrows for but to shoot? So, with the strong arms of prayer, draw the bowstring back and let the arrows fly—all of them, straight at the Enemy's hosts.[1]

God gave Jenny, our "arrow," to my husband and me to be shaped and sharpened and ultimately to be aimed and shot at evil forces in this world.

Through the years of praying for Jenny, I have seen God at work in my heart as well. I am able to release her to Him to whom she belongs.

Pray Together

Therefore do not be ashamed of the testimony about our Lord . . . but share in suffering for the gospel by the power of God, who saved us and called us to a holy calling, not because of our works but because of his own purpose and grace, which he gave us in Christ Jesus before the ages began.

—2 TIMOTHY 1:8–9 (ESV)

Heavenly Father,
I acknowledge that the children You have entrusted to us are not ours, but Yours. It is Your right to author their life story. I surrender my little arrows into Your hand, for the "purpose and grace" You have planned for them in Christ Jesus before the ages began. Thank You for the high and holy calling of motherhood. May Your will be done on earth, as it is in heaven, for Jesus' sake, amen.

When I called, you answered me;
   you made me bold and stouthearted.

                              —PSALM 138:3

Bear up the hands that hang down, by faith and prayer; support the tottering knees. Have you any days of fasting and prayer? Storm the throne of grace and persevere therein, and mercy will come down.

                    —JOHN WESLEY, *The Journal of John Wesley, Vol. 10*

Chapter Ten
Changing Schools, Communities, and Nations Through Prayer
by a mom from Latin America

KILLINGS. RIOTS. WITCHCRAFT. SEXUAL IMMORALITY. DRUG DEALINGS. VIOLENCE. THESE WERE THE WORDS IN THE NEWSPAPER HEADLINES DESCRIBING THE LARGE PUBLIC HIGH SCHOOL IN MY LATIN-AMERICAN CITY. THE SCHOOL WAS A MICROCOSM OF THE TROUBLES MANY OF THE COMMUNITIES IN MY COUNTRY FACED. NOTHING THE SCHOOL DID TO BREAK UP THE GANGS AND CURTAIL THE VIOLENCE MADE ANY DIFFERENCE.

Then I got a call from the assistant principal who had heard about Moms In Touch International. "Please," he said, "come tell us who you are and what you do. Maybe you can help us."

He asked my friends and me to talk about prayer with the parents of the most violent students at the school. These parents were required to attend the meeting, but few showed up. Those who did thought it was a waste of time. I could tell from their expressions and body language that most thought praying together wasn't a solution.

ENLISTING PRAYER SUPPORT
If those parents weren't going to pray for the school and their own children, it was time to enlist the prayers of moms who *did* believe in prayer. So at our yearly MITI event when women from different provinces gathered, we asked moms

(more like challenged them!) to pray for this particular high school, and many agreed to do so.

The following year after an onslaught of prayers from MITI members, only one act of violence was reported at that school. Next a local church was given permission to talk to kids about Jesus Christ on the school campus. As a result the students have been transformed, and there have been no more killings or gang-related acts of violence at the school for four years.

Many of the most troubled students rechanneled their energy to play in a newly organized school band. They did so well and behaved so responsibly that they were invited to march in a televised parade in the United States. Such a transformation has attracted the attention of other communities and has encouraged mothers from my country and neighboring countries to attack their schools' problems with prayer.

HOW I LEARNED ABOUT MITI

I haven't always been so bold or confident in prayer. In 1999 I was honored to be an international representative at the 15th Anniversary Celebration of Moms In Touch International at Ridgecrest, North Carolina. The fall colors at Ridgecrest enraptured me, and I was touched by the attention given to me and to the other international representatives. Oh how I wanted to learn more about this ministry! Deep in my heart I cherished the idea of being among women who prayed.

For the first two days of the training, I felt as if I were putting random pieces of a puzzle together that finally began to take shape. One thing I could see clearly: God was there and He was speaking to me through the testimonies and the beautiful prayer format I was learning.

Moms In Touch radically changed the way I pray. At Ridgecrest I learned that using the words of the Bible was the most effective way to pray for my children. I also learned how to keep my prayer focused by following the Moms In Touch Four Steps of Prayer: (1) Praising God for who He is, (2) confessing sins in silence, (3) thanking God for what He's done, and (4) interceding for children and schools. With this new prayer strategy and the leadership material, I went back to my country like the Lone Ranger, prepared and ready to fight the evil in our schools even if I had to start all by myself.

My challenge was to put this format into practice and share the blessing with others. So I started my first MITI prayer group and focused on Peter, my second child, and his school. I saw this group as a pilot prayer project. If I received answers for this troubled boy of mine, then I would call other moms to pray.

MY SON—MY PILOT PROJECT

I had three children in under three years. When he was little, Peter was emotionally attached to me. To others he appeared to be absentminded all the time, but it was not so. He was quite aware of some of the dynamics going on in our family, but too young to understand them. I was busy working and taking care of my children's educational and physical needs. As a result, I had little energy left to pay attention to Peter's emotional needs.

When my son became a college student he began showing hostility toward his father. His attitude was like an infection that was eroding our home. Peter even refused to eat at the table with the family to avoid seeing his father's face. My mother and I had prayed for a long time about this situation. But we didn't see any change.

When my Moms In Touch group started—being sure that what was shared in the group stayed in confidence—I presented my problem to the Lord Jesus, and my prayer partners supported me. They even prayed for my son during their personal prayer times. We prayed for him using Malachi 4:6 as our theme: "Lord, turn the heart of his father to Peter, and the heart of Peter to his father."

Approximately three weeks after my MITI group started praying for Peter's change of heart, my husband lost the keys to his car. When he called home to ask for help, only Peter was there. Had this happened a month before, my son would have not even taken his call, but on that day, thanks to the power of focused prayer, Peter decided to help my husband by taking him the duplicate set of keys. After they returned home, my husband initiated a conversation with our son and they actually began to talk.

Before this Peter had been withering daily as a result of bitterness, suffering from unexplainable pain that took away his appetite. But this day he was set free from physical suffering by the Lord Jesus. What started as a simple conversation has since blossomed into a loving relationship with his father. I have seen God take the words of the Bible and make them true in the life of our son, for not only has "his heart turned toward his father," and vice versa, but "today he enjoys good health and all goes well with him, even as his soul is getting along well" (see 3 John 2).

My once bitter son is now the one who strives to keep our family relationships unified. Today our acquaintances comment on his character, successful business career, and happy marriage. They call us blessed parents, and that we are. But they haven't witnessed what I saw—my son's transformation from an insecure little boy and an embittered teenager to a man of God who prays for his family and his country.

SPREADING THE WORD

Who could resist praying in a group with such a big answer in such a short time? I became convinced of the effectiveness of the MITI prayer hour and began praying about how to implement the ministry in my country. As a result, we organized a national committee of women who understood the Moms In Touch vision and began a list of others we thought might be interested. Soon we heard many stories about the wonders that God was already doing in prayer groups, and, because the news traveled fast among the women, all of a sudden we were flooded with invitations to train groups in the Moms In Touch Four Steps of Prayer format.

The ministry was truly welcomed. Everywhere we went, moms approached us and said, "This is what we needed. How come nobody thought of it before?" It took us only about two and a half years to see MITI groups praying in all the provinces of our country.

CHANGING AN EDUCATIONAL SYSTEM

One thing that's always been clear in my mind is that God is interested in blessing nations and generations. The MITI leadership in my country decided that we would not only pray for our own children and their schools, but also take every opportunity to encourage our moms to pray for the entire educational system in our country (school facilities, teachers, administrative staff, educational authorities, curricula). We wanted to see a nationwide change that would benefit the generations to come.

One of the reasons some countries like ours are called "developing" or "third world" countries is the low level of education. Such countries have poor curricula, a shortage of professional teachers, inadequate public school facilities, and a lack of technology to keep up with the outside world. As a result, parents who are financially able to do so send their children to private schools, which comprise about 50 percent of the schools in my country. That means the public schools have fewer resources and a lack of accountability. And less prayer support.

At Moms In Touch we have prayed for nine years for our country's educational problems and other cultural obstacles, asking God to allow us to see (1) our nation's children and youth receive high-quality education regardless of family income, (2) free access to education from kindergarten to high school, (3) rural schools equipped with computers, (4) teachers receiving proper training, and (5) cities freed from student violence.

It is with great joy that we constantly read in the newspapers of private companies equipping schools with updated technology or renovating a facility. The most prestigious universities now grant full scholarships for outstanding students who live in small towns and are economically disadvantaged. Additionally, in 2008 our government decreed free schooling up to 11th grade, teachers are now required to complete additional courses to become licensed, and curricula are constantly revised. Mobile libraries now visit little towns, so the once marginalized rural children have the opportunity to read, and they even have access to computers.

God's great works in our educational system are numerous, but there is one that stands out among the others: We have not heard about street riots among public high schools in the last three years.

The challenges moms face are almost the same from country to country. They all require transformation. It is this kind of transformation of children's lives, schools, and entire educational systems that inspires us to continue to encourage not only moms but also churches to conduct days of prayer and fasting for our children and schools. We know prayer is the key ingredient for the cultural changes we need in order to become the nation God intended us to be.

Pray Together

To the only God our Savior be glory, majesty, power and authority, through Jesus Christ our Lord, before all ages, now and forevermore! Amen.

—JUDE 25

———

Father,
You are a God of miracles for whom no challenge is too great! Because You know everything—the condition of our finances, the challenges in our school system, and the ungodliness in our society—You understand the fears in our hearts for our children's future. We know we can trust You with the future. Bless the faithful moms who pray so consistently for our schools. We thank You for all the answers we see. In Jesus' name, amen.

Therefore confess your sins to each other and pray for each other so that you may be healed. The prayer of a righteous man is powerful and effective.

—JAMES 5:16

To pray for [others] is of divine nomination, and it represents the highest form of Christian service.

—E. M. BOUNDS, _The Weapon of Prayer_

Chapter Eleven
Prayers Laid the Foundation for a New High School
by a praying mom in the United States

I STOOD ON THE FOOTBALL FIELD OF OUR PUBLIC HIGH SCHOOL ONE SUNDAY AFTERNOON, SURPRISED TO SEE ABOUT 200 STUDENTS AND ADULTS SPREAD ACROSS THE GRASS. THEY HAD BOWED HEADS. SOME WERE HOLDING HANDS. ALL WERE PRAYING. TWO DAYS BEFORE, A FOOTBALL PLAYER HAD GONE INTO A COMA, AFTER HAVING BEEN HIT HARD DURING A GAME AND BEING RUSHED TO THE HOSPITAL. HIS CONDITION WAS CRITICAL, AND OUR HEARTS WERE HEAVY. THE WOMEN IN MY MOMS IN TOUCH GROUP HADN'T WANTED TO WAIT FOR OUR REGULAR MEETING TIME TO GATHER. WE WANTED TO PRAY THAT WEEKEND. WE KNEW OTHERS DID TOO. WORD SPREAD QUICKLY ABOUT THE IMPROMPTU PRAYER TIME. WE DIDN'T ANTICIPATE THAT 200 PEOPLE WOULD ATTEND. NOR DID WE EXPECT THAT THE STADIUM WOULD BE FILLED WITH NEARLY TWO THOUSAND FOR A PRAYER VIGIL THE FOLLOWING WEEK. WE HAD BEEN PRAYING FOR THE SCHOOL SINCE BEFORE ITS CLASSROOM DOORS OPENED. GOD KNEW THAT THE STUDENTS, STAFF, ADMINISTRATORS, AND PARENTS WOULD NEED THIS STRONG FOUNDATION OF PRAYER TO ENDURE THAT DIFFICULT SCHOOL YEAR.

From its beginning, the high school was built on a legacy of prayer. Before I had become the co-leader of the Moms In Touch group for the brand-new school, other women had walked ahead of me—literally. Another MITI group had prayed while they walked around the dirt lot where the school was to be built. Those moms prayed that our new public high school would have a thriving MITI group.

I felt privileged to be living out an answer to their prayers.

Those first moms had prayed for a great school that would be blessed by God. They prayed that God would handpick each faculty and staff member. They prayed for the students who would attend the school. They prayed that God's presence would be evident and that His protection would be mighty. Even before the school opened, I saw God answer many of their prayers. God is amazing, and His timing is perfect!

In the school's first year, eight moms were privileged to form a Moms In Touch group and pray for this brand-new, state-of-the-art public high school. We had so much to pray for, including the new administrators, support staff, and teachers who were in charge of the many details of opening a new school.

Because the staff was all new, none of us had any idea about which teachers and staff members were Christians and which ones were not. We prayed that the non-Christian staff members would see the joy and peace found in trusting in Jesus Christ. We knew how important it would be for our school to have Christians in leadership, so we prayed especially for our principal and vice principals. Shortly after the school opened, we found out that our principal was not a Christian, so we prayed regularly for him to put his faith and trust in God. And we also prayed that the Christian staff members would spread love and hope across the school campus. We prayed they'd be encouraged in their faith and bold in reaching out to other staff members.

SHOWING APPRECIATION

An optional part of Moms In Touch International is showing God's love to the school staff through simple actions we call "Words and Deeds," gestures that provide tangible encouragement to the staff via goodies and notes of appreciation. We made an appointment to introduce ourselves to the principal. Since he wasn't a Christian, we were a little nervous he would think of Moms In Touch as a group of religious weirdos. Instead, he was receptive to us, and we left him with our contact information saying, "If you ever want us to pray for anything specifically, please let us know."

About every three months, we would have a "Words and Deeds" day. Near the teachers' mailboxes, we'd set up tables of homemade snacks and goodies. We always included a poem or some words of encouragement on the table, which was decorated in a theme. As we set up, staff and teachers often asked questions about our group. We shared that Moms In Touch's purpose was to pray for them, for the school, and for the students. Many of them thanked us personally for our prayers. Wow, did that encourage us!

The spring of our first year, the principal became a Christian. God was answering our prayers. A "hallelujah!" was in our hearts.

The following school year we continued to faithfully pray, and we planned many "Words and Deeds" events throughout the year. On the last day before Christmas break, we organized a homemade brunch outside an all-staff meeting in the auditorium. That morning the principal was so touched by our kind words and delicious goodies that he asked us to come into the auditorium for a minute. There he announced to the staff that we were a group of moms who pray for the school and that we were responsible for the goodies. The entire staff began to clap!

The following fall we were excited about continuing our group and asked the principal how we might encourage the school that year. His response was amazing: "You know what would be really great?" he said. "It would be so encouraging to me if I could pray with you moms on occasion throughout this school year." So, we began praying with the principal once a month. How amazing is that!

PRAYING IN THE STADIUM—BEFORE THE ACCIDENT

Shortly before the following school year began, a group of moms walked the sprawling campus to pray. We found ourselves praying in the bleachers of the deserted football stadium. It seemed we prayed even more specifically than usual for the year's upcoming sporting events and student participants. A few weeks later we realized how lovingly God had prepared us with this sweet time of prayer for a great difficulty ahead. It was during this period when one of our school's varsity players collapsed on the field and was rushed to the hospital. After the game, the hospital was packed with concerned teammates and coaches. They were devastated to learn that this player was in a coma and that his survival was uncertain.

On the following Sunday afternoon, a Moms In Touch leader spoke to a large group gathered at the football field. She then divided us into smaller groups to spread out onto the field to pray. Students, teachers, coaches, and parents circled together, with each group led by one of our MITI moms. We prayed for the injured player, for a miracle, for healing, for his family and friends, for the football team and coaches, and for strength and wisdom. I felt a strong sense of God's presence on that football field.

ORGANIZING A PRAYER VIGIL

Over the next week, concern and love for this injured football player and his family poured forth from the students, staff, and community. Even other schools across the county began calling our school to see how they might help. The hospital room where the injured athlete lay in a coma had a steady stream of concerned and praying visitors. It was an emotional, sad, and difficult time for everyone involved. So, again our Moms In Touch group, along with our school principal and a local community church, decided to do something out of the ordinary. We organized a prayer vigil to be held on the football field that Sunday, just a little over a week after the accident. We asked youth group leaders from several local churches to speak. We also asked our principal, a few students from local schools, and two of the moms from our group to speak.

I was one of those moms. Each speaker was to share something specific from their heart about the reason we were all together, and then lead a time of prayer for a specific group, such as the football team, the coaching staff, the school staff, the parents, the students, and the community. I was to pray for our students. Having never done anything like this before, I was nervous, but I was also moved to see how God was touching this school and community.

Word spread quickly, and almost two thousand people showed up to pray. Entire football teams and cheerleading teams from other schools came. When it was my turn to speak and pray, I introduced myself as the co-leader of the high school's Moms In Touch group, and I explained that we meet regularly to pray for the school and the students. "Life can be difficult and scary," I shared, "but we have a big God that will be with us and give us courage and strength. If we believe in God and trust Him, God will never leave us nor forsake us." I asked all the students to stand up, and I prayed for them. It was difficult not to cry while I spoke, but I really felt God's strength during this time. We never dreamed that God would bring so many people together to pray for a public school.

STUDENTS BEGIN PRAYING

Over the next weeks and months, our Moms In Touch group spent extra time in prayer for this injured young man and his family, and we continued to witness God at work. Students posted big signs across the school fences asking for prayer for this young man. For the first time at that school, it was cool to pray. God opened doors by allowing spiritual things to be acceptable to talk about on the school campus. Students were wearing handmade bracelets that encouraged prayer for this boy. Even the community supported this family in amazing ways: Local businesses got involved in fundraisers to help with medical expenses. Neighbors, friends of the family, and several local churches organized events to support the family, including providing meals for many months following.

During the sixth week, the injured player "woke up" from his coma. Even though he still was in critical condition, it was a miracle that he was alive. As a group we rejoiced that God had answered our prayers. The teen gradually got well enough to move from the intensive care unit (ICU) to a therapy floor of the hospital. Then he was eventually moved to a hospital nearby that specializes in brain injuries and therapy. About seven months after his injury, he was finally allowed to go home. He still has a long road of recovery ahead of him, but he is making progress, and we continue to pray for him and his family each time we meet.

His younger brother was extremely distraught over his brother's tragic condition. He was also confused about the outpouring of love from the school and community. Why were strangers caring for him and his family? I was able to talk and pray with him just days after his brother's injury. Over the following months, Christian teens reached out to him and invited him to church. Within a few months of his brother's injury, he accepted Jesus as his Savior.

ASKED TO HOST BACCALAUREATE

By the end of the school year we had built such a trusting relationship between our Moms In Touch group and the school that several on the school staff asked if our group would host a baccalaureate at the end of the year. So, with great privilege and honor, we co-hosted the first ever baccalaureate for our high school graduating seniors. We had tremendous help and support from the same church members who came alongside us for the prayer vigil. About 40 graduating seniors participated in the ceremony, and it was a sweet time of dedication and prayer for them. We hope to continue this as a tradition for each graduating class in the coming years.

The school's fifth year began with amazing news. Not only did we have a Christian principal, but we now had Christian vice principals, as well. We praised God again for another answer to our prayers! Then the principal shared that he and another administrator had started a prayer group with other Christian principals, assistant principals, and district administrators. The group meets once a month for prayer and to grow in servant leadership. Just a few years ago, our principal did not believe in a personal God, and now he is organizing leadership prayer groups.

BEING STRONG AND COURAGEOUS

We have seen God at work in numerous and amazing ways in the four and a half years we have been praying for our school. Through it all, there have been times that were so painful and discouraging, but we continued to trust God and He has been faithful to respond. Joshua 1:9 commands us to "be strong and courageous. Do not be terrified; do not be discouraged, for the Lord your God will be with you wherever you go." There is no doubt that God has gone before us time and time again as we continue to lift up our high school and our students to Him in prayer. It has been a wonderful privilege to be part of this Moms In Touch prayer group, where I learned to pray like never before. There is something so powerful about praying together with other moms for our own children and for our school. To see God at work so faithfully, in such amazing ways, is a beautiful experience.

Pray Together

[A Pharisee asked Jesus,] "Teacher, which is the greatest commandment in the Law?"

Jesus replied: " 'Love the Lord your God with all your heart and with all your soul and with all your mind.' This is the first and greatest commandment. And the second is like it: 'Love your neighbor as yourself.' "

—MATTHEW 22:36-39

Dear heavenly Father,
You are our Wonderful Counselor, Mighty God, Everlasting Father, and Prince of Peace. May Your love shine through each Christian mom and pour out onto the school staff and community. Please give them Your wisdom and compassion when faced with struggles and tragedies. May their words and actions reflect Your grace, and may they truly love others more than themselves. In Jesus' name we pray, amen.

If any of you lacks wisdom, he should ask God, who gives generously to all without finding fault, and it will be given to him. But when he asks, he must believe and not doubt, because he who doubts is like a wave of the sea, blown and tossed by the wind.

—JAMES 1:5-6

Pray and never faint, is the motto Christ gives us for praying. It is the test of our faith, and the [more severe] the trial and the longer the waiting, the more glorious the results.

—E. M. BOUNDS, *Purpose in Prayer*

CHAPTER TWELVE
WHEN CHILDREN DON'T BOND WITH THE FAMILY
by a California mom

*M*Y HUSBAND AND I PRAYED FROM DAY ONE THAT OUR CHILDREN WOULD HAVE "BORING TESTIMONIES"—THAT THEY WOULD BE HAPPY, BALANCED KIDS, WHO LOVED GOD AND THEIR FAMILY. OUR DAUGHTER GREW UP WITH A DELIGHTFULLY BORING TESTIMONY AND IS HAPPILY MARRIED WITH CHILDREN OF HER OWN. HOWEVER, HER BROTHERS—IDENTICAL TWINS—CHOSE A MUCH MORE COLORFUL PATH.

I knew my second pregnancy was very different. Even though my doctor insisted there was no medical verification of twins, out they came. Little did I know the double trouble ahead for our precious preemies!

For almost two years, John and Paul were on a liquid-only diet and suffered from screaming pain, chronic diarrhea, and exhausted parents. By the time they turned three, we were so relieved to have finally found two meats, two vegetables, and two fruits that would stay in their systems. Within another year, the boys' health and diet were pretty normal. However, their emotional scars were deeper than we ever imagined.

About 20 years later, we were told that children with severe pain in infancy may not bond with family members, because they associate the cause of their pain with the faces they see. John and Paul did not bond with us, their older sister, or each other. When a child does not develop loving, trusting relationships within a family in early childhood, most everything in life becomes distorted and, as a result, all discipline and structure may be resented.

Although the boys, especially Paul, really wanted to feel loved and accepted, there was an invisible wall, an inability to bond that kept them feeling isolated and unloved no matter how much we sought to fill their emotional tanks with tender touch, affirming words, and focused attention. None of us understood what was happening. We just saw an ever-increasing anger, frustration, and rebellion simmering within the boys that erupted in screaming tantrums. Unfortunately, Doug and I often added our own rage to these volatile outbursts, making the invisible wall of detachment thicker and thicker as time went on.

GROWING FURTHER APART

"But John, we are one of God's wonders," was Paul's sweet reply when four-year-old John vehemently complained about having a twin. From preschool on, John resented Paul for "being his shadow," even though they were in separate classes. To make matters worse, their neighborhood friends could not tell the boys apart so they called them both "John-Paul." That way they were at least half right, but it only infuriated John even more. So we color-coded the boys. Paul wore red and had a red bike. John had blue everything. The boys even had separate birthday parties. Finally, Red Paul and Blue John had their own identities. How I wish that had solved all their problems!

By the time John and Paul were in elementary school, they were "two cats in a bag," not "two peas in pod." Life became an exhausting social, academic, and athletic competition. "Anything you can do, I can do better" was not the half of it! There were also constant problem-solving meetings with teachers, coaches, and scout leaders. Their older sister, Kim, was as embarrassed by her brothers' behavior as we were.

We moved to a new community when the twins were in fifth grade, and John made it abundantly clear that Paul was not to spend time with any of his new friends. This division was even stronger in high school, when John and Paul played different sports. John's rejection hurt Paul very deeply, launching a downward spiral of depression in him that we did not recognize for years because it was hidden behind his anger and resentment toward us.

Throughout middle school and high school, John and Paul excelled academically, athletically, and as Eagle Scouts. However, we were spending more and more time dealing with ever-increasing discipline, drug, and legal problems at school and with the police. This certainly was beyond my abilities to cope or resolve. Only God could handle all this!

Spiritual Equilibrium in Ever-Increasing Trauma

Fortunately, I had met Fern Nichols when John and Paul were in fourth grade, and from then on I eagerly participated in Moms In Touch groups at our daughter's school and the boys' school. My weekly MITI groups became my lifeline of hope for the next 10 years. The fellowship of other praying moms, the many answers to our prayers, and our constant focus on the attributes of God held me in spiritual equilibrium during the ever-increasing trauma of John's and Paul's choices in middle school, high school, and college. It always amazed me how God would refresh me during our MITI prayer times, no matter how heavy the burden or how hopeless the situation appeared. Praising God for His attributes and thanking Him for everything (anything!) I saw Him doing kept me in peace despite the emotional and legal chaos around me.

Things came to a head when John was arrested for drug dealing his sophomore year at college, and an angry Paul came home a few weeks later for what we called the "Christmas from hell." The loving support of my MITI sisters carried me through Paul's rage, explosive departure, and months of silence, as well as John's trial, sentencing, and jail time. In the midst of all this chaos, God was at work answering our prayers that John and Paul would "feel loved" and "get right with God."

John was truly humbled by his arrest and trial, as well as by the loving support he received from us and the members of our church. But we were disappointed and confused when he specifically asked us to stay away from his final sentencing hearing. Later that day we reached his attorney by phone, and he said, "I am really mad at John—but you will be proud of your son!" Wanting a truly clean slate, John had confessed to several offenses, things that could never be proven against him. His confession freed a friend from jail time, but it extended John's sentence to six months. Amazing!

One Son Returns

A few months later at college, Paul had an intense encounter with God that would change him forever. Paul described his experience as being "engulfed by God's love" and "having an insatiable hunger for God's Word." All the verses he had learned in childhood moved from merely words of theory to actual, unalterable truth. The message of God moved from his head to his heart. All the scriptures I had prayed week after week at MITI suddenly became a vivid reality for him. Paul was so transformed that he came home from college to ask our forgiveness for all the pain he had caused us.

I will never forget the many tears of joy at my college MITI group the following spring. Paul asked me to wear a special Mother's Day T-shirt he had made for me. He also wanted me to thank all the MITI moms who had prayed for him and John since sixth grade. The T-shirt had a picture of Paul praising God and John reading his Bible. The caption read, "Prodigals Return, God Hears Prayer." Amen!

God has done an amazing healing work in Paul's heart. Paul asked our forgiveness for all the ways he had dishonored God and us over the years. Paul also sought help for his depression and his difficulties in bonding with others. And today, he is joyfully serving God.

Unfortunately, John never cleaned his spiritual house the way Paul did. Although he was active at church and talked about Jesus with others for over a year after his release from jail, John never dealt with his past pain, unforgiveness, or deepening depression. Once again, John's choices became increasingly more colorful and painful: resentment, drugs, jail, psychiatric intensive care units (psych ICUs), living on the streets, and increasing isolation due to depression, agoraphobia, and panic attacks.

We did everything we could emotionally, medically, and legally to help John without enabling him. Eventually, he cut off all communication with us. Later we heard John was living in an old 1976 van. For five years, we joyfully received his parking tickets as confirmations that he was still alive somewhere in our city. We rarely knew where he was or how he was doing. His silence was deafening.

In May of 2006, we entered a new world of pain when John attempted suicide. By God's grace, he is alive. After another visit to the psych ICU, John spent 14 months at a Christian men's ranch, more in body than in spirit. When he was finally forced to leave, John was homeless once again. You can imagine our shock when John, then 32, called us on Labor Day 2007 and asked us to come get him. It had been seven l-o-n-g years since John had chosen to see us.

John was "homeless" at home for the next 13 months, rarely speaking or bathing. My dear MITI friends and many others prayed for us as we loved and served him unconditionally for a year. Then he disappeared without saying good-bye and cut off all communication once again.

Currently, there is encouraging progress with John. Paul invited John to visit him and check out a Christian program for transforming the homeless into productive citizens. We are praising God for every encouraging report about John that we hear from Paul and others since he joined the program two months ago. God is still at work!

GETTING THROUGH IT

I am often asked, "How do you keep going year after year, despite the painful silence, constant rejection, and many unknowns surrounding your son?" My husband and I have been in this deep, dark valley for almost two decades. We certainly do not claim to have all the answers, but we have made many helpful discoveries that enable us to joyfully live by God's spiritual light and continue to enjoy a fruitful life in the midst of our pain. We are eager to encourage other hurting parents. We could never have handled our pain alone!

I am blessed with a godly husband. The glue that has held Doug and me together through this long, painful journey (and many other challenges) is our commitment to pray together every night. We have not missed many nights of prayer in our 41 years of marriage, except when we are geographically separated. The one-accord praying I learned through MITI revolutionized how Doug and I pray together. This process is praying back and forth about one issue until we sense there is nothing left to cover. We now take turns leading so we can hear each other's heart and concerns. Because we established this pattern when we had fewer problems, it has enabled us to weather the storms in unity, when so many things were seeking to tear us apart.

HOW I'M CHANGING

During the boys' early rebellion, I desperately needed to connect emotionally with God in the midst of my pain, confusion, and sense of failure. I knew I would be shooting myself in the foot if I tried to survive this mess without spending time daily with God and by reading the Bible, His very words. I realized that if I read slowly, verse by verse, and asked God to stop me when He had something He wanted me to know, stop, change, or do, He would help me navigate each day.

I began to change, not my circumstances. After a while I began journaling the things God was showing me in the Bible each day. It has been such a joy to go back through my old journals and see all that God has done as I have prayed through the whole New Testament and much of the Old Testament over the years. I often note specific answers to prayer in purple, God's royal color. On my down days, I can quickly find encouragement and hope by rereading my purple praises. This has truly become a prayer time I do not want to miss!

My "survival" scriptural principle is found in 1 John 1:7: "If we walk in the Light as He Himself is in the Light, we have fellowship with one another, and the blood of Jesus His Son cleanses us from all sin" (NASB). I cannot be in fellowship with Jesus if I am out of fellowship with anyone else. This requires me to confess my sin and make things right if I have offended others, as well as forgive anyone who has offended or hurt me. During my daily prayer time, I mentally picture all the key people in my life, asking God to show me if I need to confess any sin or forgive any hurt, so I can "walk in the Light" with Him.

I must *often* forgive John for the pain, fears, and frustration his choices cause me, because I will not let my hurt block my relationship with Jesus. I can also be in a relationship with John—there is no barrier coming from my side—even though he is unwilling to acknowledge me. My intimacy with God provides the continual emotional and spiritual support I need to face each new challenge.

I cannot change John. Only God can. I can change only myself—no one else! This has helped me to see that this whole adventure with our sons has been more about changing me than changing John and Paul.

MITI has been a tremendous part of the change in my life. Through the safety of MITI, I learned to be open and honest before God and others. I also discovered the power of focusing on God's characteristics and praying Scripture for myself and my family.

Praying one to one, heart to heart, with another mom was a transforming experience that has helped me in practical ways in many other relationships as well. Many of my MITI sisters have remained faithful prayer partners who are only an e-mail away. I praise God for my many MITI friends who are still praying for John 10 years after college.

What would I do without the support of those praying moms!

Pray Together

God may grant them repentance leading to the knowledge of the truth, and they may come to their senses and escape from the snare of the devil.

—2 Timothy 2:25-26 (NASB)

O compassionate Father,
I pray that You would flood the minds of moms of troubled children with Your grace and peace. Please comfort these moms and sustain them so they don't give up! Give them the courage to continue praying that their children will escape the lies that keep them fearful, bitter, and angry. Replace those feelings with Your hope and joy. In Jesus' name, amen.

Let us draw near to God with a sincere heart in full assurance of faith, having our hearts sprinkled clean from an evil conscience and our bodies washed with pure water. . . . for He who promised is faithful.

—HEBREWS 10:22–23 (NASB)

———————

The prayer of the feeblest saint on earth who lives in the spirit and keeps right with God is a terror to Satan. The very powers of darkness are paralyzed by prayer . . . no wonder Satan tries to keep our minds fussy in active work till we cannot think in prayer.

—OSWALD CHAMBERS, *Christian Discipline, Vol. 2*

Chapter Thirteen
Unlocked: Hope for Moms with Disabled Children
by Thalia Henning of California

FOR YEARS MY PRAYERS FOR MY PROFOUNDLY AUTISTIC DAUGHTER, KOREN, CENTERED ON THINGS LIKE SAFETY AND HAPPINESS. SHE COULDN'T SPEAK OR COMMUNICATE WITH US IN ANY WAY, AND LONG AGO I GAVE UP HOPE OF KNOWING WHAT SHE MIGHT BE THINKING OR THAT SHE COULD UNDERSTAND MY WORDS OF LOVE TO HER. THE FRUSTRATION WAS AWFUL—HOW COULD I KNOW WHAT SHE WAS FEELING? WHEN SHE GROANED, WAS SHE HUNGRY, UNHAPPY, OR IN PAIN?

Koren is my third daughter. In 1981 she was born at the Keesler Air Force Base hospital in Mississippi, in a birthing room that had never seen a delivery. Koren was the first.

When a pediatric team came in to evaluate her, I was relieved to learn that she checked out completely normal and healthy. Yet I had had problems with my second daughter right after birth, and I examined Koren carefully. I asked my husband, Pete, if he thought she was quivering. He didn't see anything that concerned him.

Signs of Trouble

Though her birth went well, I realized early on that Koren wasn't developing normally. She smiled often and her blue eyes tracked movement, but her chubby baby legs just hung instead of curling up. And she was unable to use her hands like most babies. It wasn't until she was 10 months old that the reality of Koren's condition began to surface.

117

That day Koren was napping, and I was working in our garage. Alexis, my eldest daughter, came to tell me the baby was crying. I found Koren in her crib, in the throes of a seizure. I had seen my middle daughter, Dena, have seizures from high fever, but this was different. This seizure continued.

On the way to the hospital I was frightened, yet I was also surprisingly calm because I knew I couldn't do anything more. I prayed to God and told Him I understood that Koren belonged to Him. I would not worry, but I would trust in Him to accomplish whatever plans He had for her, be it life or death. It was a faith-filled prayer, but I nevertheless finished with "Please let her be okay!" God answered my prayer right away, because Koren was awake and alert by the time we got to the hospital. But it wasn't the complete healing I had hoped for.

Instead doctors diagnosed Koren with cerebral palsy. She began occupational therapy at 20 months. Eventually the doctors rediagnosed her as autistic and severely retarded. They said her intelligence quotient (IQ) was around 17. The specialists suggested we put her in an institution because her capabilities would not progress beyond those of a toddler.

One day when we were at a family gathering at the swimming pool, a relative and I were watching our children play happily. I was shocked and hurt when that relative said in all seriousness, "I really think you should send Koren away. She might grow up to hurt our boys or other kids." But we wanted Koren to stay with us. We were a family. We knew God had not made a mistake when He gave Koren to us. We knew He had a purpose for her.

GLIMMERS OF GOD'S PURPOSE

At two and a half, Koren walked like a little penguin, fluttering her hands at her side. When we were Christmas shopping that year, a homeless man came up to us and said, "Now look at that! She's dancin'!" Not wanting to go into the details, I simply agreed. He smiled and watched her for quite awhile. She smiled, too, and never cowered from him. Finally, he reached into his pocket and handed me a dollar.

"Take this and buy something for her for Christmas."

I felt I should have been giving *him* something, but I could see it would rob him of a blessing if I didn't accept it.

"Okay, I will. And thank you," I said. We went immediately into a store where I bought her a clip-on Santa that we still put on our Christmas tree each year. That Santa reminds me that God has a purpose for Koren's life despite her limitations. That day He used her to bring joy to a stranger simply because she was not afraid to interact with him like other children might have been.

By the time Koren was five years old, we had moved to Hawaii. She was smiley and cute, with long brown braids and an intelligent expression on her face. We often questioned her diagnosis because, though she couldn't speak or follow directions, she would sneak out of the house or take something she wasn't supposed to have, all the while managing to avoid anyone who might notice. Plus, as she got older, we could tell that she could always remember how to get places. She was just so trapped in her body and, unfortunately, we tended to accept the professionals' opinions.

When she was six, the first-grade Sunday school teacher at our church asked if I would like Koren to attend. No one had ever offered to teach her before. In class Koren wouldn't stay seated. She flapped her hands and made guttural sounds, but the teacher never complained. This was such a blessing to me, and later on we saw so clearly how it was part of God's plan.

In Hawaii I heard about Moms In Touch International and joined a group that prayed for Dena's high school. Later the Navy sent us to Virginia, and I prayed with another group of moms.

GOD'S PLAN UNFOLDS

In 1996 we moved to California. My husband went ahead of us to pick our neighborhood, Koren's school, and her teacher. Koren, who was now 15, entered a special education class at our local public high school. And I went looking for a Moms In Touch group.

As God had planned it, some moms at Koren's new school were having an informational coffee to start the first ever MITI group for that school. There I met Janelle and Adrienne, my first two friends in California, and we began praying together right away at my house. Immediately, I could see that God had hand-placed me.

We had a small but active MITI group. We prayed diligently for the school and regularly took goodies and fun surprises to thank the teachers, staff, and administration for their service to our kids.

Most of my prayers for Koren dealt with safety and happiness. All my new friends were praying for tests, proms, driving, and homework. Yes, sometimes it was almost unbearable to sit there with no hope for any progress in Koren's life. And when Dena gave us our first grandchild, I couldn't help thinking how sad it would be to watch him grow and develop past Koren's abilities.

But God had a plan, and He used our MITI group. During that first year, one mom came periodically to our group. She didn't know us well, but God, through His Holy Spirit, led her to pray for Koren to "meet her full potential." As she prayed out loud, I remember thinking, *She just doesn't get the full picture of Koren's limitations.* But God began answering that woman's prayer.

After 14 months of praying together in my MITI group, we saw an incredible miracle. Koren's teacher said she believed Koren had a motor planning problem, not unlike a stroke patient, and wasn't retarded at all.

"I want to try something with Koren," she told me. "It's called 'facilitated communication.' It doesn't have a high success rate. In fact, it hasn't worked with any of my other students, but I think it might work with Koren. Do you want to try it?"

She explained to me that she, or a trained facilitator, would push back on Koren's hand to add resistance as Koren attempted to point to an object, picture, or letter. The procedure was new at the time and quite controversial, because there were questions about whether the subject was actually doing the choosing or just being guided. But it certainly wouldn't hurt her, and we thought it would be worth a try.

After years of little progress, *in one short day* Koren was unlocked!

Miraculous revelations followed rapidly. Over the next few days we found out Koren could read at the college level and do math in her head. She had a sense of humor and strong opinions. Once she could communicate (one finger at a time), she had a lot to say. Several years later she wrote this about the experience:

> My teacher told me she wanted to try a way to help me communicate. Truly, I didn't expect much, but when I saw that she was doing something so different from what I had seen before, I dared to reach for a much forgotten desire to create a sweet bond with the wanton world I had given up on. Quickly, Joan took my hand and resisted the reach as I reached for the fresh trials she set before me, deciphering the words by reaching toward one letter at a time as she asked me questions. I was able to spell out yes and no and then spell out my name this way.
>
> The exuberance I felt truly hampers my explanation of it, and I seem to need a good thesaurus to freeze my feeling into words. Tremendous joy and startling freedom overtook my body as I realized I was going to finally be known for who I really am. The attitude toward me changed quickly. I was now getting lots of attention and some deserved credit for my brain, and I freely received the greased wheel of education as my future.

The best news was this: Koren told us she knew that Jesus was her Savior and she had accepted Him into her heart at age six in Lynn's Sunday school class. She typed that Jesus had told her she was a fine child and He loves her just as she is.

HOPE FOR AN ACADEMIC FUTURE

The following year Koren started high school as a real student. During her high school years she wrote for the school paper and developed an interest in journalism. Here is one page from her journal:

> The excitement continued each day as my teacher assessed my knowledge and savvy, trying to determine what to do with me now. Yesterday, she saw me as a retarded, autistic teenager, but now she was facing a challenge she had never met. What to do with a severely disabled girl who is also quite intelligent, but unable to speak or treat her body as others do?
>
> We decided to have me start ninth grade the coming September and what a change that was! Treating me now as an equal member of the ninth grade, friends started to come to me slowly, marveling at my abilities. My school days were filled with required courses that ensured a diploma. The first year I took five courses, including English, Algebra, and Spanish. For the first time I sat in academic classes, filling up on sweet knowledge, treated as any other learner, and expected to freshen up my thinking skills. The classes were fun and enthralling. I loved going to school. Dances, football games, and homework were now part of my school experience, and I felt that I finally was dreaming no more.
>
> One of the dearest changes was being on the school newspaper and writing several articles during the two years that I took journalism. I was respected as part of the others and saw that I had a future somewhere in writing, seeing for the first time I had something meaningful I could do with my life. My life wasn't perfect and I still heard students conversing about my weirdness, but finally I knew that many people saw my intelligence, so I was able to dismiss the wounding words and study on. I eventually went on to graduate with a 3.82 GPA.
>
> Truly, this change was the most awesome surprise! Once I could

type and show the world who I really am, school became an exciting chance to learn and express my thoughts.

The highlight of Koren's life was her high school graduation day. She graduated with a real diploma, feeling it might be her entry into the world, but it was sadly not the stepping-stone she hoped it would be. She did go on to attend community college for one year with me acting as her assistant, but it became difficult to continue. The faculty was skeptical of her intelligence in light of her odd behaviors; the staff also questioned whether or not Koren was really doing all the work or if I, as her facilitator-mother, were helping her. It would have been difficult to find another facilitator, but the issue didn't come up. The community college banned her from having a facilitator at all during exams, which made it practically impossible for Koren to be evaluated.

WHAT DOES THE FUTURE HOLD?

We're at a crossroad now. Koren is 27 and would love the freedom that usually comes with age, including the joy of driving a car. But she wakes up in a home where all the doors need to be locked so she won't wander off. Her days are boring, and she spends most of her time with me. Nearly every day she eagerly waves the car keys in her hand to encourage me to take her out to "see the sights." And I do, as often as possible.

I've cried over all the years wasted, wishing I knew then what I know now, but I don't feel guilty. All those years Koren was growing, we did all we knew to do for her, including showering her with constant love and attention.

We continue to hope she'll fulfill her potential and find her purpose in life. She has had some opportunities to go to schools and "speak" to children. She's using a machine now that actually gives a voice to her typing, though she doesn't much like the sound of it. She explains to kids what it's like to live her life and how much God loves them. She wants to write more, have more interaction with friends (though the nature of her disability makes real camaraderie a challenge), and go back to school. We want those things for her, too, and will never stop searching for ways to make them happen.

I see God's hand every day in my family—from Alexis's chosen profession as a special education teacher, to Dena's nursing career and six years of praying with Moms In Touch, to Koren's gift of being able to put her life into words, to all the people who love, pray for, and help us.

This is my hope and prayer for her: that the God who created her and loves her and knows the details of her life will continue to show her the purpose He has planned for her.

The entire six years that I was in high school I was prayed for. I knew that Moms In Touch prayed for me every week even before God released me from the awful, sad bondage in my body. I was dreaming of waking to a world where everyone could see weighted ideas from my own mouth, but awesome God woke me with facilitated communication. Thanks to God and dedicated moms, I received life that clearly meant a new deep reason to be here.

Thank you Moms In Touch for having moms pray. I sweetly felt each prayer. I knew what the moms wanted but could not have. They wanted treasured God to completely heal me, but I was given freely reasonable thoughts and sweet breathtaking moments with awesome God.

Freely keep praying for your children and grandchildren.

Pray Together

[The Lord] said to me, "My grace is sufficient for you, for my power is made perfect in weakness." Therefore I will boast all the more gladly about my weaknesses, so that Christ's power may rest on me. That is why, for Christ's sake, I delight in weaknesses, in insults, in hardships, in persecutions, in difficulties. For when I am weak, then I am strong.

—2 CORINTHIANS 12:9–10

Dear Father,
We praise You for "unlocking" Koren! For every child who feels trapped in an unwilling body, Lord, we pray You show him/her that You have a spectacular purpose for his/her life. Surround us mothers with caring prayer partners who will lift our needs before You, who will pray the bold prayers, and who will remind us that You are with us in all things. In Jesus' name, amen.

He will call upon me, and I will answer him;
  I will be with him in trouble,
  I will deliver him and honor him.

—PSALM 91:15

———————

No prayer is too hard for Him to answer, no need too great for Him to supply,
no passion too strong for Him to subdue; no temptation too powerful for Him to
deliver from, no misery too deep for Him to relieve.

—ARTHUR PINK, *The Attributes of God*

Chapter Fourteen
Enduring a Child's Open-Heart Surgery
by Kim Vinson of Florida

I WAS IN EMOTIONAL AGONY. MY PRECIOUS SON, ALLEN, WAS ONLY NINE YEARS OLD, YET I HAD TO FACE THE REALITY THAT HE MIGHT NOT SURVIVE HIS SECOND OPEN-HEART SURGERY.

I couldn't fathom the idea of losing a child. How does a mother bear this burden? Would I ever again hear his laughter? Would I miss the challenge of answering his questions? Would the joyful silliness between him and his little sister be silenced? And what about the future? Would my husband and I rejoice together over Allen's high school graduation? Help him pick a college? Attend his wedding? Was this it? Was this the summer when we would slip from "family of four" to "family of three"?

The burden was too heavy to carry alone. My lifeline was a Moms In Touch International group that often prayed for Allen's upcoming surgery. Through prayer and God's amazing grace, I found the courage to be strong for my son.

When I first started attending Moms In Touch, I would not utter a word. I was praying fervently in my heart but was too shy to pray out loud. Slowly, I began to feel comfortable enough to pray out loud.

At each meeting we first read one of the Bible verses about an attribute of God. Then, we have a time of confession, which, thank goodness, is always done in silence. Next, we offer thanksgiving to God. Then it is time for intercession, time to pray on behalf of our children and school. I say "our" children because we have developed a special bond by praying weekly for every group member's children. We share our innermost desires and wants that only another mother can truly understand. Meeting to pray one hour weekly has made such an impact on my life.

Just before our MITI group broke for the summer, my mom friends and I circled together and prayed for Allen and his future. I found great comfort in the prayers that were lifted up on his behalf. That day each woman there seemed completely confident Allen's surgery would be a success. I found hope in their confidence.

Allen was born with an abnormal aortic valve. This was going to be his second surgery to correct it. Our carefully selected surgeon was to perform the complicated Ross procedure, a surgery in which the aortic valve is first replaced with the patient's own pulmonary valve. Next the pulmonary valve is replaced with a manufactured valve.

If Allen survived, this new valve would need to be replaced about every seven years. He would need another surgery at age 16 and then again every seven years or so thereafter.

REASSURING ALLEN, WHEN I WASN'T SURE MYSELF

We struggled to reassure Allen that he would be okay. But I didn't believe my own words. I tried to act confident as I answered each of his questions, but inside I was struggling with the same concerns. He wanted to know: "What if the surgeon makes a mistake?" "How am I going to feel after the surgery?" "Why was I born this way?" and "What if it *is* the will of God that I die?" With each question, I silently prayed, asking God to help me answer in a way that would calm Allen's fears. But my fears were not calm. My heart was racing, and I was worried.

Knowing that my Moms In Touch friends were praying helped bring me peace. Before the surgery, I was presented a list of almost 70 people who had committed to pray for Allen and the surgical team for 12 hours the day of the surgery. The list had 24 half-hour time slots and indicated which two to three people had committed to pray for us during each interval. Words cannot express the comfort my family found in knowing we were not alone in our vigil.

"THE HARDEST THING I'VE EVER HAD TO DO"

When Allen was wheeled into surgery, my husband, John, said aloud what I was feeling inside: "Letting go of Allen is one of the hardest things I've ever had to do."

Questions plagued my mind: *Would the open-heart surgery be too hard on his little body? Would he survive? And if he did, would he recover fully? Or would Allen always have physical limitations?* I needed to bring my worries to God, so my mom and I slipped into the hospital chapel, the same chapel where we had prayed for my father before he died. I tried not to let my mind wander to my father's death. Instead I clung to the knowledge that even if something went wrong during surgery, everything would be all right because we could trust that God was working in our lives. Of course, that was easy to tell myself but much harder to put into practice. I found great peace in knowing that God would never leave us and He would continue to sustain us even if we couldn't lift ourselves up.

But the fear returned as soon as I walked back to the waiting room. Through the window, I could see Allen's cardiologist, dressed in scrubs, in deep discussion with John. I felt as if the wind had been knocked out of me and our greatest fear had come true. I assumed Allen had not made it through surgery or there had been some complication. I held my breath as I opened the door. They both looked up at me. Surprisingly neither of their faces looked sad or worried. They seemed happy. I knew it was too soon for the surgery to be over, and I waited for more information. Then the cardiologist excitedly shared what the surgeon had discovered in the operating room. This surgeon, whom we had prayed that God would handpick, said he didn't need to replace Allen's aortic valve because it only needed to be repaired. That occurs in only 5 percent of such cases. Five percent.

God was answering the prayers of those faithful prayer warriors.

But time was of the essence. John and I needed to make a quick decision. Did we want the surgeon to try to repair the valve or do the more complicated Ross procedure? The surprising news took time to settle into my mind.

All I could manage to ask was "This is a good thing, right?"

"Yes!" said the cardiologist, repeating it over and over again: "Yes! Yes! Yes!" His emphatic answer broke the tension, and we all began laughing with sheer joy.

My husband and I announced, "Yes! Have the surgeon try the repair!"

The cardiologist went running off to relay the decision to the surgeon. Then I called the first person on our prayer chain, who then spread the good news. We were all rejoicing together! This was the miracle we had prayed for.

FEELING HELPLESS

I felt a great relief—for the moment. After the surgery, when Allen was finally brought to the intensive care unit (ICU), I had to hold back my tears. Wires and tubes snaked across his little body, making him look as if he were prey trapped in a spider's web. I barely recognized my little brown-haired boy. But worst of all, he was in *extreme* pain.

"Mommy, help me! Please help me!" he begged over and over, his sweet face tense with agony and fear. I had never felt so helpless.

The nurse asked, "How much pain are you in on a scale of one to five?"

Allen's answer: "Five!" He was turning to me for help, and it sickened me to know I was powerless to fix this. I was thankful the doctors could give him medication to lessen the pain, but I will never forget that heartrending moment.

As Allen recovered, I couldn't help but remember my father, who endured a long stay in that same hospital. The memories flooded back as I thought about that harrowing time nine years ago, when I spent many days with my dad, until he died. Just seven weeks after my dad's funeral, Allen was born.

But it was not the joyful event I had expected. The day of his birth, Allen was whisked away by Flight For Life and brought to this same hospital. The place where my father had suffered, my son then suffered, surviving his first open-heart surgery as a tiny infant. Now we were back again in the hospital's ICU.

But this hospital stay had a more joyful and unexpected ending.

NOTHING SHORT OF A MIRACLE

On the evening of Allen's surgery, his pain subsided, and he actually sat up in a chair by himself. We praised God and thanked all our faithful prayer partners. On day two Allen surprised us all: He was off pain medication and was well enough for the drain tubes and exterior pacemaker wires to be removed. He was actually up walking around the ICU with nurses, family, and monitors in tow! And on day three, just 72 hours after open-heart surgery, he was completely untethered from all monitors and was able to go home and sleep in his own bed!

The speediness of his recovery left me awestruck. I knew we were experiencing another miracle. Allen had been the exception. He surprised the doctors and nurses, who started calling him The Cardiac Kid. Allen amazed us again when, two weeks later, he was out on the tennis court hitting balls with his father! God had granted us the miracle the MITI moms had prayed for.

God used this experience to work on my heart as well—my spiritual heart. Through all of this, I have developed a closer relationship with God, deep-seated in prayer. In my MITI group, I had learned and memorized some attributes of God that I could emotionally cling to while I was filled with fear.

What a joy it was for me to pray with my Moms In Touch group again after Allen's surgery that summer. I had seen the profound impact of answered prayer, and I couldn't wait to express my appreciation to God during the thanksgiving portion of our MITI prayer time.

Answered prayer also had a great impact on Allen. Experiencing the miracle of quick healing strengthened Allen's faith and was a tangible example of how much the Lord Jesus loves and cares for him.

ALLEN PUTS HIS FAITH IN CHRIST JESUS

Though Allen and I had often talked about Jesus, I wasn't the one who asked him to make a commitment to trust Jesus' offer of eternal salvation. I'm delighted to say it was a classmate. Right in the middle of the busy school cafeteria, surrounded by watching peers, Allen bowed his head and prayed with his friend to become a Christian.

Allen's boldness of faith continues to be obvious on campus. Allen, who was age 10 at the time, and a group of boys began taking turns saying grace before lunch in the cafeteria. What a good example those afternoon prayers were to the adults and classmates who overheard them! The boys were never asked to stop, and their boldness influenced a table of girls from his class to begin saying grace, too.

Just a year before, I had been struggling to discern God's will in Allen's health situation. Now I can see that God used the surgery to show His power to others. Allen's perseverance throughout his ordeal was a confirmation of the power of prayer. He has continued to grow both physically and spiritually, boldly declaring his faith. In a schoolwide speech contest, he told about his open-heart surgery experience. His closing paragraph read as follows: "In about 10 years I know I am going to have another heart surgery. But next time I will not be as worried or as nervous because I learned a valuable lesson from my experience. I learned that when you face a challenge in life, never give up or be afraid of the unknown." Allen knows that God is with him and that He answers prayers.

LOOKING TOWARD THE FUTURE WITH HOPE AND CONFIDENCE

Yes, Allen will need another heart surgery sometime in the future. But I know God has a plan, and I have learned to patiently wait on Him. Some days are better than others. I struggle with fear of the unknown and wish I could know what the future holds for Allen. We travel to see Allen's cardiologist twice a year, and with each visit we leave relieved there isn't any change in his heart. At least, not his physical heart.

Allen is now 12, and I'm pleased to say he looks like a typical middle school kid. Our family continues to grow closer and closer. Our sweet-spirited nine-year-old daughter, Anna, made a Christmas card for her brother. In it she wrote: "God has blessed you. You're full of happiness." When Allen was a young boy, each night he would end his prayers with "and please take care of my heart, God." Now he ends his prayers each night with "Thank You for taking care of my heart, God."

Pray Together

Even though I walk
    through the valley of the shadow of death,
I will fear no evil,
    for you are with me;
your rod and your staff,
    they comfort me.

—PSALM 23:4

Dear Lord Jesus,
Comfort the moms of critically ill children. Give them Your guidance and wisdom. Surround them with a supportive prayer team who offer all their emotional burdens to You, the God who hears and cares. Bond their family together in unity as they walk through the agonizing and perplexing maze of medical appointments, tests, and decisions. May they feel Your peace even as they "walk through the valley of the shadow of death." In Your holy name, amen.

You will keep in perfect peace
    him whose mind is steadfast,
    because he trusts in you.

—ISAIAH 26:3

Prayer is not a collection of balanced phrases; it is the pouring out of the soul.
—SAMUEL CHADWICK, *Twenty-Five Sunday Mornings with Samuel Chadwick*

Chapter Fifteen
My Heart *Still* Sings
A Mom Faces Her Child's Suicide
by Connie Kennemer of California

On November 17, 2005, Todd Kennemer, my beautiful boy—the recipient of 25 years of my prayers, love, and devotion—bid farewell to his broken world and hello to his perfect and painless eternity. Moms' stories are always wrapped up with their children. So Todd's story is my story, too. And my declaration, like Jonah in the Carl Sandburg poem "Losers," is "I came out alive after all."[1]

Todd, the Songbird

Todd was our songbird from birth. Music was his conversational tool and he used it constantly. My husband and I often commented that he got both of our musical genes, plus one of his own. When Todd was three, I accompanied him as he charmed our congregation singing the Joel Hemphill song "He's Still Working on Me." When he finished to rousing applause, he stood up on his stool on the platform, took careful aim, and jumped. Never a dull moment with a creative child!

Todd studied violin from the age of seven and grew to be an accomplished player, but his real passion was the guitar. His love for worship still gives me pause as I recall accompanying him on the violin, watching him lead worship, listening as he led classmates in praise, worship, and prayer at such school events as See

You at the Pole. Music was Todd's language, his love, his life. How I prayed that God would use this gift for His holy purposes.

In the mid-1980s when Todd was five, my husband and I felt God calling us to transition from a full-time church music position to work in a small mission agency based in Southern California. The area we settled in had a nationally renowned school district, a lifeline for parents who wondered if entrusting their treasures to the public school system was a good idea.

As a first-time school mom, I hovered over Todd, offering to be room mother right away. Spending too much time in Todd's classroom probably overexposed me to anything and everything that could set off internal alarms. And those alarms rang often during Todd's first school year, like the day another classmate had to stay inside at recess for using the f-word—in *kindergarten*! I vaguely remember quietly sobbing on my bed upstairs that afternoon. *Lord, is this life in San Diego? If so, may we go home now?*

God's answer came within a matter of weeks when a mutual friend introduced me to Fern Nichols. At that point, I knew nothing about Moms In Touch International; I just knew I needed help right away. I can envision the scene like it was yesterday: I am praying in a room of total strangers who are all passionate-for-God moms of high schoolers. I have a five-year-old son, and *my* only prayer is how to get him out of California as soon as possible!

In retrospect, that first introduction to Moms In Touch left me longing, curious, and captivated by how this group of women prayed. I was drawn to them and drawn to Fern, this humble woman leading our prayer time. After the hour, I introduced myself to Fern and explained my plight. Her response was immediate: Start a Moms In Touch group at Westwood Elementary School! *Me? Start a group? In a town I don't know, in a school I don't even like?* I knew the answer before I even formed the questions. *Yes, you. Nothing is impossible for the woman who believes.*

Thus the first Moms In Touch group was birthed in the elementary school I grew to cherish. And, in turn, Westwood Elementary grew to cherish this small band of women who prayed for their children, prayed for their teachers, and lovingly, regularly, brought goodies into the teachers' lounge. And what was birthed in me, the leader? A fresh and growing fervency to pray with other moms with similar concerns and to praise God as I came to a new understanding of His many attributes. I also learned the critical importance of maintaining confidentiality in prayer time, something I have taken into every prayer setting since my first MITI experience.

I hail this marvelous group of cookie-baking mothers, this now worldwide organization, as my school of prayer. I am still attending that school.

So Todd's young life was accompanied by his parents' commitment to prayer, via Moms In Touch. My husband, Rex, often tells his friends this: "Connie and I walk around the block, and she just starts praying. And she naturally expects me to agree in prayer with her!" Rex may joke about it, but it's been his school of prayer, too.

Todd's True Heart

This was the atmosphere Todd grew up in. Not a seamless setting, I assure you. But the air in our home was scented with prayer—many times, prayers of repentance because of our foibles as parents and the ways in which our words and decisions wounded Todd. Wouldn't we all like do-overs when it comes to raising our kids? But God is and always has been the perfect parent. I learned so much about God's character and faithfulness in my weekly Moms In Touch times. Rex and I clung to those divine attributes when we were in over our heads.

Todd made a commitment to Jesus Christ before he was five years old. He loved the Lord very much and told everyone he knew about Jesus—even San Diego Padres baseball great Tony Gwynn. Always a talkative boy, he probably did his share of sinning with his words (much like his mom). But he also used his words to heal, and I still treasure an e-mail I received from Todd during his first year in college.

I had just sent him an article I had written regarding my journey with multiple sclerosis. Todd's healing words were these:

> I got your letter today with your article. I tried to read it to my friend as we left the post office, but I broke down halfway through the second paragraph. THAT'S MY MOM. Mom, I am sorry for all the times I've argued over dumb things with you while you're battling fatigue and just the will to keep going. I am sorry for the grief I have caused you by not humbling myself before you when I should have. I wish I had dropped out of school and just protected you wherever you went. I guess I am trying to tell you that I love you very much.

Even a decade later, his words bring me joy because they reflect Todd's true heart.

It's critical for me to remember Todd's true heart as I revisit the events of the last three years, events that swirl through my mind several times every day and threaten to swallow me. Before Todd's death, I wrote a curious reflection that came from deep within my heart. I could only term what I penned a eulogy, though I didn't know for whom. For Todd? For me? I *still* ponder that question. Less than six months after writing it, Todd took his own life after a cruel and crushing battle with bipolar disorder. I miss Todd with my every breath and heartbeat, but I rest knowing he is free from the torture chamber his mind had become. My spontaneous but prophetic tribute was included in his memorial program:

"I LOVED MY SON."

Write on my gravestone—
Say it in my eulogy.
Speak it simply,
Tell it truly—
I loved my son.
Don't regale songs I've sung
Or tales I've told
Or carols I've crafted.
Only this: I loved my son.
The air is sweet, but silent now—
Just breathe a blessing,
Proclaim the prayer that is eternal,
And needs no amen.
Ponder the holy pause, the *selah*;
The legacy that lives on
For time and eternity:
"I loved my son."

Some of my mental and emotional fog has lifted since Todd's heavenly homecoming. I now understand this puzzling tribute. It is a prophetic whisper from heaven. I would make only one small change to reflect the present: The air is sweet, but it is *not* silent. The atmosphere is filled with the voices of a thousand friends, with music, laughter, tears, and memories that will enrich all of our lives . . . until we see God face-to-face and our Todd close at hand.

Where Was God?

Even with the waves of tributes that were paid to Todd and to his Christian influence at his memorial service, his death was a crushing blow for us with painful implications. Why *us*? Why *now*? Where was God?

I'd been asking this for over a year before Todd's illness was evident and diagnosed. My grieving began during the phone conversation in which he informed me that he no longer considered himself a Christian. Along with my son's vibrant faith, a part of me died that day. My MITI friends joined me in praying for Todd and other children who have turned their backs on God. There were moments when MITI prayers were my only lifeline.

We prayed that our prodigal children would come "to [their] senses" as did the lost son in Jesus' parable (Luke 15:11–32; see especially verse 17). We prayed that Todd would see the Father running to meet him. The lyrics of Todd's childhood chorus rang through my mind: "He's still working on me." There is a New Testament verse written by the apostle Paul that echoes and affirms that song: "[God] began a good work in you [and] will carry it on to completion until the day of Christ Jesus" (Philippians 1:6). The term "good work" refers to the holy redemption process of a person who has accepted Jesus Christ as his or her Savior.

I won't know until heaven what led Todd to pull away from God. I am forever clinging to Jesus' words in the Gospel of John that He will not let any of His "sheep" be snatched from His hand (10:28–30).

My Faith Crisis

After Todd's death, I entered a season of grief along with a serious crisis of faith. I was disoriented by the disorderly place into which I had been dropped. I was angry that I had to live here now—I didn't even want to *visit*. Thus began the reshaping of what I really believed. I realized that I had erroneously let my faith become a formula: If I did my part, God was obliged to do His. Obedience results in blessing—the phrase was familiar but flat in light of Todd's death. *I had led Moms In Touch groups since Todd entered kindergarten; this wasn't supposed to happen to me!*

It was in this deep darkness that my only connection with God was through the hands, feet, words, and touch of church members, collectively called the "body of Christ" in the New Testament by the apostle Paul. I was reminded by my Moms In Touch leader that on the day of Todd's death, we praised God as our Deliverer. The leader's words still ring in my heart: "Connie, God answered our prayer! God delivered Todd!"

Only loving friends—the old analogy of "Jesus with skin on"—could help, and help came in waves, flooding over Rex and me. I couldn't go to Moms In Touch for several months after Todd's death, so they came to me, bringing food, music, hugs, prayer, laughter, movies, books, and memories. When I could read Scripture again, I read psalms that reflected the laments my soul was experiencing. So many of the psalms written by King David of Israel voiced the heartache I felt. David's pain authentically mirrored all the emotions that seethed in me—anger, disappointment, disbelief, abandonment, physical and mental pain. For example, Psalm 13 opens with the cry of my heart: "How long, O Lord? Will you forget me forever?" I felt forsaken and forgotten.

But Jesus met me in my rage with the compassion and empathy that only One who had been forgotten and forsaken could. I tried to freeze Him out, but my long-enduring love relationship with my heavenly Friend thawed the ice. I could not weather this devastation without Him by my side. The disciple Peter's response to Jesus in John 6:68 was my response: "Lord, to whom shall we go? You have the words of eternal life." I needed my Savior.

DIFFERENT AND THE SAME

Six months after Todd's death, Fern Nichols asked me to give my testimony at a Moms In Touch retreat. It was the first public place where I talked about what Rex and I had been going through. I knew that it was imperative to tell Todd's story—our story—to the women I had walked with, worked with, prayed with, loved our children with. They were waiting to hear from my lips that I was still standing firm—or at least limping purposefully—even when the floor was in shambles beneath me. I said to them what I say to everyone who asks me, even now, three years later: Is it still difficult? Yes, as difficult as trying to hold one's breath indefinitely. Painful? Every mom knows it is.

What has changed? Life as we know it has changed profoundly and will probably continue changing for a long while. Some of the changes have enlarged our souls, equipping us to help others. Some have tormented us for a season. Some have pushed us deeper and transformed us in ways that better reflect both the character and the compassion of Jesus. That's good.

But overarching all this is what has *not* changed. The promises of God in His Word (the Bible) have not changed. Jesus has not resigned His job as the heavenly Intercessor—He's still with the Father, sitting at His right hand, praying for us (Romans 8:34). The devil hasn't changed. He's still the "father of lies" as

Jesus calls him. He's a thief intent on killing, stealing, and destroying (John 8:44; 10:10). The battle against evil and spiritual despair hasn't changed—our need to engage in spiritual warfare by praying remains critical. And we are more in need of wearing our spiritual armor than ever before.[2] God's presence in my life hasn't changed. His promise to never leave me or forsake me is the same (Hebrews 13:5; Deuteronomy 31:6), just not as tangible as I would like it to be (that, too, will change). The power of prayer hasn't changed.

What E. M. Bounds said many years ago rings in my ears: "God shapes the world by prayer. Prayers are deathless . . . they live before God and God's heart is set on them. . . . Prayers outlive the lives of those who uttered them, outlive a generation, outlive an age, outlive a world."[3] The important things, the eternal things, have not changed.

Carl Sandburg's poem "Losers," which I referenced at the beginning of this chapter, is my story: I was "swallowed once deep in the dark / and came out alive after all" in full view of God's glory and amazing grace.

AMAZING GRACE

Grace is the word that is woven throughout my life now. The grace of God to give Rex and me such an amazing, fascinating boy. The grace to be three years beyond tragedy and still standing. The grace to, as Oswald Chambers says, "come face to face with the deepest, darkest fact of life without damaging our view of God's character."[4]

Grace was one of Todd's favorite words. At the close of a period of his life spent ministering to San Francisco's homeless teenagers, he created a crude stencil and spray painted "grace" throughout his beloved neighborhood—the sidewalk on the way to his favorite coffee shop, a corner claimed by gangs—reminding the homeless and those who care for them that life is not all dark. That faded graffiti still adorns the sidewalk in the Mission District of San Francisco. Friends who live in the area still walk by it and remember. I can never forget this final act of creative vandalism that Todd left in a neighborhood that will have his graffiti on their hearts—on *my* heart—forever.

The thought that "prayers are deathless" is branded on my heart and validates my passion to pray for *other* mothers' sons and daughters. It took me awhile to return to my Moms In Touch group, but my desperate need to be reminded of *who* God *is* drew me back. There is no other arena in my Christian life that has better acquainted me with God's character. Now I spend the first hour of every

Thursday morning praying with the group that carried me through my "valley of the shadow of death" (Psalm 23:4).

I close this chapter by reflecting on my core belief regarding my wonderful son, Todd: He is with His Savior, and checking out *our* rooms (John 14:2) in the new heaven, the holy city (Revelation 21:1–2). I have asked God if our room could be close to Todd's, because we have a lot of catching up to do.

The school of prayer is still in session. I am more convinced of that fact than ever before. Todd, my prayers for you live on. I anticipate our heavenly reunion when I will see your toothy smile, hear the tenderness in your voice, and muse over what color your hair is now. Todd, we *knew* it would end with our heavenly Father keeping the promise He made in Revelation 21:5, "I am making everything new."

Psalm 118:17 is our anthem until we meet again, my son.

Pray Together

I will not die but live,
> and will proclaim what the LORD has done.

—PSALM 118:17

———

God,
Our hearts break for the mothers who have lost their children. Comfort their hearts. Restore their hope and joy in You. Heal them. Love them. Envelop them in the aroma of sweet memories. In Your holy name, amen.

If you live in Me [abide vitally united to Me] and My words remain in you and continue to live in your hearts, ask whatever you will, and it shall be done for you.

—JOHN 15:7 (AMP)

———————

There is no way that Christians in a private capacity can do so much to promote the work of God, and advance the kingdom of Christ, as by prayer.
—JONATHAN EDWARDS, *Narrative of the Revival of Religion in New England*

Chapter Sixteen
Healing for Victims of Sexual Trauma
by a Mississippi mom

I remember the fun weekends when my daughter, Adriana, and I would go with my husband to a marathon, sightsee in the city, and then attend the after-race celebration. We'd also take "mystery trips" as a family, for which one parent would choose a destination, and all that the others were told was what to pack. We didn't know where we were going until we got there. And we loved our frequent family bike rides along the river and our weekend outings to the zoo.

I always considered myself a good mom and thought I did everything right. I even worked from home so I could be there for our daughter. We were active in church and were a close family, never missing Adriana's recitals or a youth group activity that parents were invited to. We guarded what our daughter watched on TV and thought her Internet access was monitored, even though she had a computer in her room. Despite all of this protection, Adriana was sexually assaulted—raped—by someone she knew when she was 15.

How did she get entangled in the relationship with the predator?

Evil reached out to our daughter right in our home, while we were there but unaware of what was happening.

INSTANT MESSAGING MENACE

I used to think Instant Messaging (IM) was fairly innocuous if we knew the people Adriana was contacting. I felt savvy because I knew one person could IM multiple friends simultaneously. What I didn't realize, however, was that every computer screen interfaces with every other computer screen. This means that while your child simultaneously communicates with three friends, those three could be simultaneously communicating with multiple other people. Therefore, your child can end up Instant Messaging someone 12 people removed, someone your child has never met.

I also had no idea how dangerous it was for Adriana to keep her cell phone by her bed at night. Unbeknownst to us at the time, she talked on her cell phone, sometimes all night, with the man who would eventually sexually assault her.

One night while my husband and I slept, the man called her cell phone and asked her to open the door. When he began to violate her, she didn't call out for help because she was more afraid of getting in trouble for sneaking him into our home than she was of being sexually assaulted. Our hearts broke as much over our daughter's lack of trust in our ability to champion and protect her as over what the man did to her.

THE BROKEN PIECES

The next three years were a fog of self-recrimination and debilitating depression for my entire family—me, my husband, Adriana. Though she was unable to articulate her feelings as such, her behavior said it all. Sexual assault leaves adult women feeling guilty or helpless, disenfranchised in relationships, angry, and cynical of sex. Their self-esteem is also crippled.

When a young woman is raped, these effects are multiplied a hundredfold. So it was for my beautiful daughter. Even her appearance changed to reflect her grief and anger. She began tweezing her eyebrows to give a harsh, edgy impression to her face, but the external wasn't where the change was most noticeable. She went from a vibrant sophomore high school girl who wrote sing-song happy rhymes she recited to me so we could giggle together, to writing black, hopeless, vulgar poetry about death and destruction, drugs, and sex.

She'd been a gifted artist, illustrating blank books with a colorful world of fairies with lacy wings and gossamer gowns. But after the assault, all the color went out of her art. Exit fairies. Enter demons, skulls, and four-inch black tarantulas. I often wept when I saw the new entries in her sketch journals.

Her speech changed dramatically as well. Our formerly articulate honor student began talking like a stranger, taking God's name in vain every other sentence, and cursing at her dad and me. She'd always had a good sense of humor, but she didn't laugh for months on end except when mocking me or ridiculing someone's misery on a TV drama.

While she blamed herself for the sexual assault, a part of her also blamed us for not waking up to rescue her. So she took out much of her rage on us. In the next year, her circle of friends began to shift from the wholesome kids she'd known most of her life to a much more disturbing demographic. The daughter who used to be emotionally close to me and share what was going on in her life became secretive and hostile. She tried to commit suicide twice. She was in and out of adolescent psychiatric wards, and we spent thousands of dollars on counseling, yet nothing seemed to help her.

Feeling Alone

I began to feel ostracized from my church. Mothers of my daughter's former church friends began avoiding eye contact with me and cutting me glances from the corners of their eyes. Nobody called to find out why my daughter stopped attending Sunday school or youth group functions. We were in severe pain and our daughter in crisis. Yet instead of love and compassion, I felt judged, misunderstood, abandoned, hung out and left to dry.

If you've raised your daughter in a church and prayed for her, she doesn't get sexually attacked, right? Christian families don't have children who attempt suicide, right? As my daughter's former church friends spread the word about what had happened, parents seemed to don social biohazard suits to protect their families from what surely must be a contagious and deadly virus they might otherwise catch from me and my daughter. I felt desperately alone.

I began to believe the lies of the enemy who incessantly whispered: "You failed. You are a terrible mother. Your daughter is better off without you. In fact, the world is better off without you." I even started to plan my suicide.

Yet God saves even while we are in our pit of despair.

I found out that "God is faithful; he will not let you be tempted beyond what you can bear. But when you are tempted, he will also provide a way out so that you can stand up under it" (1 Corinthians 10:13). The way God provided for me to stand up in the midst of this horrible tragedy was through Moms In Touch International.

My sister called one day and suggested that I go online to find out about Moms In Touch, an unusual recommendation since she wasn't even a member of the group. I learned that the MITI state coordinator lived less than a mile from me. I called her that day, and she graciously invited me to her home. The first meeting, I went with my Bible slippery in my sweating, nervous hands. *Would I be rejected again? Would I be ostracized because my daughter had been a victim of a sex crime?*

Those first few months in Moms In Touch are a blur to me now, but I remember weeping a lot. Sometimes that's all I could do. I wasn't able to participate in any meaningful way because I was so shattered and broken. Though I was the only one with a child who'd turned away from God, not one woman judged me or Adriana. They all accepted me and loved me the way I was, and they cared about my daughter enough to pray for her, not just once but every week. That meant everything to me.

THE TOUGH TIMES

Through the faithful prayers and tender acceptance of my Moms In Touch friends, I began to learn that God did not judge me for my child's choices, and He did not blame me for not rescuing her while she was being assaulted.

During all this time, my husband had to take a job in another city and could come home only on weekends. Though in a committed marriage, I was for all practical purposes a single parent—and frightened. In her senior year, my daughter declared war on me. She stopped obeying me, shouted "Shut up!" when I spoke, and began throwing things at me and hitting me. Since I knew she was doing drugs, I bought a home drug testing kit and insisted on her testing clear before she could go out with friends. She quickly found ways to sabotage the drug tests and finally refused to take them at all. At five foot ten, Adriana was no longer a child I could physically restrain.

Once after she had tested positive for drugs, I told her that she couldn't go out.

"I hate you so much I would kill you if I thought I could get away with it!" she hissed at me. Then she left and slammed the front door behind her.

All alone, I cried myself to sleep on the stairs, waiting for her to come home, but she didn't that night. I became afraid of my own daughter and her threats of murder. With my husband having to live near his job, I was alone most of the time. Our bedroom door didn't have locks, so at night I wrapped his leather belts around the two handles of the double doors. I had become a captive in my own house.

FROM BAD TO WORSE

Flight attendants on airplanes explain that in an emergency, the parent is to put an oxygen mask first on herself and then the child. Otherwise the parent may pass out, leaving the child with nobody to protect him or her. When the emergency happened in my family, God knew I needed an oxygen mask for myself first so that I could be effective for my child. The prayers in those first couple of Moms In Touch years did not appear to change my daughter, *but they did change me.*

I've found that when we engage in diligent prayer, we alert the enemy that we are fighting back. And when we subsequently come under even greater attack, it's merely proof that our prayers are making a difference, not that we're failing!

For me this meant that things at home went from bad to worse. On February 17th my husband was coming home to celebrate a late Valentine's Day because he had been gone on the 14th. I thought the three of us could have a wonderful meal together, maybe patch things up with our daughter and start over. Hope floated my heart as I cooked all afternoon in anticipation of my husband's arrival and all three of us being together again. Finally everything was ready, and I called my daughter to the table for dinner. She shouted vulgarities, refusing to join us. Her dad asked a little more forcefully, and things began to escalate. Being high on drugs, she refused to eat the meal already prepared and instead stomped in the kitchen, opened the freezer, and grabbed a frozen pizza.

When I stepped in the way of the microwave, saying, "No. Eat what I fixed or go hungry," it was like a powder keg had been ignited. Adriana shoved me away, slapped me, and started clawing at me like a wild animal. I struck her back in defense, and in the blur of the next few minutes, the police arrived (my husband had called for help to subdue Adriana). Both my daughter and I, with bloody noses, were arrested, put in separate squad cars, and booked at the police station. After taking my fingerprints and photographing me, the police talked with me and my daughter in separate rooms. Later that night they let me go home.

However, Adriana was not allowed to come home. In fact, authorities told me I couldn't have any contact with her or even come within 500 yards of her for many months. Instead of being put in state custody, she was allowed to live with family friends and finish high school.

During this devastating time, state child custody officials came to my home and interrogated me to ascertain whether or not I had abused Adriana. I faced the possibility of jail time if the courts determined I had. Even though I was found innocent, it was one of the most humiliating, lonely times of my life.

I remember a social worker coming to my house at one point to "investigate our living conditions." She told me she needed to document that my daughter had her own room and provisions. I suppose she thought I might be such a monster as to make my child live in a box in the garage. At first I felt very defensive, but it turns out this was a kind woman—and that was God's grace to me, too. We ended up sitting on my couch, and I began to weep and tell her our story. She was a soft-spoken woman who'd seen her share of pain, I could tell. She told me one of her young sons had died just a year before. Then she told me something I still cling to: "As long as they're alive, there's hope."

GRADUATION BRINGS DISASTER

Even after Adriana graduated, there were no positive signs in her life. In fact, she started dating an older drug dealer, who was seven inches shorter than she was but made up for it with bravado and bullying. Rather than having a criminal's appearance, he looked like an athletic, well-dressed Abercrombie & Fitch model. But his behavior was violent and manipulative. He gave her a kitten and then threatened to kill it if she didn't do what he said. Then he began calling her foul names and beating her. He threatened to kill her on more than one occasion.

Our Moms In Touch group doubled our prayer efforts: God was *not* going to let the enemy have this one! I had moments of horrible fear, like when Adriana moved out of her apartment to get away from him. Though I wasn't there (by court injunction), witnesses said he shoved her to the sidewalk, twisted her arm, and ground her face into the pavement. A girlfriend of hers who saw it happen called an ambulance because Adriana's injuries were so bad and she was in so much pain.

In times like these when I didn't know where my child was, I realized God knew. He has seen where she was, where she is, and best of all, where she will be. No matter how far the distance or how dark the shadow, I learned there is no place a child can go that God is not present and with her (Psalm 139:7–10). He sees her eternity, and He will never forget her.

I realized then that because the devil's attributes are the opposite of God's, whatever the devil whispered was the exact opposite of the Truth. God gave me wisdom so I could understand that my suicidal thoughts were lies straight from the pit of darkness (John 8:44).

This meant that when I was despairing of life, plotting my suicide and thinking that my daughter would be better off without me, *the truth was that my daughter was* not *better off without me.* She needed me more than ever—especially as her prayer intercessor, a mother's most important and powerful role on this earth. The evil one knows this, too, and that's why he'll go to extraordinary lengths to disable us, keep us unceasingly busy or distracted so we don't pray for our children. I thank God nearly every day for this revelation because it imbues me with renewed determination to pray for my daughter without ceasing (1 Thessalonians 5:17).

Those first three years were my "Moms In Touch Boot Camp" years because that was where I learned to listen to God. Sheep know their shepherd's voice and follow it (John 10:27). The day came when I could finally say I was thankful for my daughter's rebellion because through it I learned—for the first time in my life—to identify my Shepherd's voice and how to follow it. I remember when He spoke to me that "perfect love drives out fear" (1 John 4:16-18), and because of my aware-ness of God's perfect love for me and my daughter, I stopped "panic praying" and started "power praying."

Around Christmas every year my MITI leader hosts a candle-lighting prayer time for our children, in which each candle represents not just our child but also Christ's light in them. Around the room as each mother prays out loud for her child, she lights a candle. My third year in MITI, I went prepared to pray for my child as usual. That day, my Shepherd's voice urged me to also pray for her drug-dealer boyfriend. My daughter had a split lip, and part of her face was still on a sidewalk where he had stomped on it just a few days earlier. Pray for *him*—this violent, drug-dealing abuser who had viciously beaten my daughter? I had every excuse ready not to.

Yet I knew my Shepherd's voice by then, so I did as He asked. I honestly told God I was saying the words but needed Him to help me mean them. The day I began praying for my daughter's abuser was the day their relationship began to change. My daughter began to see the dangers and vile choices this young man was encouraging her to make. All of us in my MITI group celebrated this and other answers to so many prayers. I was buoyed and hopeful! I thought surely now we were out of the proverbial woods.

Satan prowls as a formidable lion, however, and does not relinquish prey lightly once he finds it (1 Peter 5:8). My daughter went from dating a drug dealer to moving in with a woman who introduced her to prostitution through an escort service, the primary client being a prominent citizen in our hometown. My husband and I learned this man owned several party mansions in a tourist resort on the ocean and would fly young women there in his private plane, plying them with drugs to lower their inhibitions. Every time we'd read another article in our newspaper about this "wonderful" prominent citizen, we would alternately weep and shake with rage.

Our Shepherd's voice calmed us by telling us to turn this over to the FBI and to trust Him to protect our daughter through the authorities (Romans 13:4–6). God reminded me of the lesson about praying for the drug dealer: I began to pray for this prominent citizen exploiting our daughter. I learned that love is victory. Jesus didn't endure His crucifixion because He knew He could get revenge when He rose again. He did it because through that ultimate act of love, the enemy was defeated.

God showed us to ask Him to help us love our child's enemies *so that Satan's plans for her would be defeated.* What He commands us to do, He equips us to do (Hebrews 13:21), and so He did in the life of me and my husband.

Fast-forward five years. Does my daughter now ask us to hold hands and sing "Kum Ba Yah" or talk of God's redemptive power in her life while dabbing at her moist eyes with Kleenex (cue the violins)? No. Not yet.

Does she even go to church at all? Ever? No. Not yet. We're still in the middle of many struggles, but there are many big and little ways God graciously lets me see that prayers are being answered. Our daughter no longer prostitutes. She's been in the same stable relationship with a gentle young man for over a year. It's been many months since she's hung up on us or used foul language in our presence. Every time we speak on the phone, she tells me, "I love you, Mom."

I've learned that for us parents of prodigals, God wants us to never give up praying for our dear one. The evidence of her restoration may seem sparse or nonexistent, but even while she is still a long distance away, her Father sees her coming just as the father of the prodigal son in Luke 15 saw his wayward boy coming down the road.

Our daughter's story isn't over, and God is still at work. Though I know I have made mistakes, I can have peace knowing that God is the only perfect parent and He can and will *make everything right* in His time.

Pray Together

I am still confident of this:
>I will see the goodness of the LORD
>in the land of the living.
Wait for the LORD;
>be strong and take heart
>and wait for the LORD.

>—PSALM 27:13–14

Dear Father,
Please heal the hearts of all moms whose kids are not following You. Help each mom focus on You and persevere until the breakthrough comes. I pray for the power of Christ to tear down all the works of darkness in the lives of our children. Deliver them from the power and persuasions of the evil one. Please pour out Your incredible goodness in their lives, and lead them to You, Your forgiveness, and Your love. In Your precious name, amen.

O Sovereign LORD, you have begun to show to your servant your greatness and your strong hand. For what god is there in heaven or on earth who can do the deeds and mighty works you do?

—DEUTERONOMY 3:24

———

The ultimate end of all our prayers is that God be glorified.
—JOHN MACARTHUR, *MacArthur Daily Bible*

Chapter Seventeen
WHEN CHILDREN AND MOMS ARE HURT BY DIVORCE
by a California mom

LIKE A MASSIVE EARTHQUAKE THAT ROCKS BUILDINGS OFF THEIR FOUNDATIONS IN MINUTES, JANUARY 2003 SHOOK MY LIFE TO ITS FOUNDATION AND CHANGED EVERYTHING. IN THE WAKE OF ONE MORE EPISODE OF MY HUSBAND'S INFIDELITY, I LEFT MY LOVELY HOME AND MOVED INTO A TINY APARTMENT, BEGINNING YEARS OF COMPLICATED DIVORCE PROCEEDINGS. MY THREE ADULT CHILDREN, UNAWARE OF THE CIRCUMSTANCES AND CONFUSED AND HURT BY THE BREAKUP OF THEIR FAMILY, PULLED AWAY FROM ME. I LOST MY HOME, MY FAMILY, AND ALL THE SECURITY AND COMFORT I'D KNOWN FOR SO MANY YEARS. EVERY NIGHT AFTER WORK, INSTEAD OF COOKING A GREAT MEAL FOR MY FAMILY AND GETTING TO HEAR ABOUT EVERYONE'S DAY, I ATE BY MYSELF IN MY LONELY KITCHEN.

A few months before my personal upheaval, my son, Will, had returned from four years as a firefighter in the Air Force. With a new wife to support and the dream of completing his college degree, he accepted his father's offer to work for his corporation. It seemed a perfect solution at the time, but it also placed Will in close contact with his dad, who used every opportunity to lie about me and excuse his sexual infidelity. When I finally got up the courage to leave, Will cut off all communication with me, and our relationship went from bad to worse.

Each of my children handled the breakup of our family differently, crumbling in his or her own way. I wasn't the only one wounded: We were all hurting,

157

and in our pain we did what it took to heal. My daughters dealt with either anger or depression. But we still had a relationship, strained as it was, and we were able to talk and work through the heartbreak together.

But with Will it was only silence and isolation. One afternoon shortly after Christmas, I saw him towering above the crowd in the parking lot of our neighborhood grocery store. The relationship between us had become so cold that when I approached him, he totally ignored me. He was wearing the Christmas present I had left on his doorstep a few days earlier. Seeing him in the navy blue cashmere sweater I had handpicked for him was the only proof I had that he received the gift—and proof also that he couldn't be too mad at me or he wouldn't be wearing it.

Within weeks of seeing him in his new sweater, I learned Will had quit his job at my ex-husband's corporation to take a position as a firefighter with a large government contractor. The drawback: He was being sent to Afghanistan. I called him and sent e-mails asking to see him before he took off, but to no avail.

The day before he left I drove by what was once our family home where his dad now lived with his new girlfriend. I saw Will sitting on the steps petting the dog so I pulled the car to the side of the road and called to him.

"I heard you were leaving. Are you going to say good-bye to me?"

I didn't expect him to respond, but he stood up—he was wearing his classic "uniform" of board shorts and T-shirt—and he ambled down to the eight-foot wrought-iron fence that lined the property. He didn't open the gate, but stood there opposite me, not looking me in the eye. We said good-bye. No hugs, no kisses—just an indifferent good-bye, followed by my one quiet plea to "stay safe." I could tell he was uncomfortable, and he occasionally glanced back to the house as if to make sure his dad or girlfriend didn't catch me near the property. My heart was broken. I was broken. Will was broken.

MOMS IN TOUCH TO THE RESCUE

My relationship with Will has always been delicate. He was *not* an easy child to raise. I always said that God gave me two hands, and both hands had to be on Will at the same time! I often thought that when Dr. Dobson wrote the book *The Strong-Willed Child,* Will's picture should have been on the cover.

I worked in his classroom when he was in grade school and signed up to be team mother when he played sports, but it was usually to keep tabs on Will and make sure he didn't get into trouble. Being constantly on the alert with him was a big responsibility for me and one that I tried to handle on my own. I admit I grew frustrated and tired with the burden. Will was a typical teenager and was growing tired of me, too, and our frustrations scratched and dug at our relationship.

When Will started high school, I was called often by a teacher or principal about his behavior. Although his infractions were not serious—like not doing homework, talking too much in class, or the occasional cutting class with his friends—I continued to worry about him, the choices he was making, and the friends who were influencing him. I worried if he would go to college (especially with his low GPA), and I wondered what he was doing when I wasn't around. This burden was becoming increasingly heavier, and I knew I couldn't carry it myself; yet at that time I felt I had no one to turn to.

It was then, in 1993, that I heard Fern Nichols on the radio and was introduced to Moms In Touch International. MITI seemed to be an answer to my need to share my concerns with someone who understood.

At my weekly Moms In Touch meeting, I learned how to take a scripture verse, put my kids' names in it, and so "pray the scriptures" for my kids. And I learned to pray out loud in a group. This was new for me, and at first I was uncomfortable, but with the encouragement of the other moms I kept coming back to the weekly meetings. I saw God carry us through the normal stresses of high school and college, then Will's tour of duty with the Air Force.

In my Moms In Touch group I discovered that I could take everything I was worried about and tell it all to God through prayer. I learned that "perfect love casts out fear" (1 John 4:18, NASB) so I didn't have to fear for my children's future because God loved them more than I did and He would give them "hope and a future" (Jeremiah 29:11). I also found I wasn't alone—I had other moms praying alongside me. I learned to pray for the big things like college entrance exams and driving for the first time. I also learned that God was interested in the little things, such as when I prayed that Will would do his homework or obey his curfew.

AFGHANISTAN

When Will left for Afghanistan, I had no idea it would be nearly three years before I would see him again. I would learn of trips home for vacations and holidays, but he never called and rarely returned my occasional e-mails. I vacillated between sadness, anger, embarrassment, and confusion, along with the ever-present guilt, as I watched the disintegration of my family's relationships. I felt helpless as I saw my children hurt and go through the painful healing process. I clung to God's promise that "He heals the brokenhearted" (Psalm 147:3, NASB). I felt God had personally promised me that I would see my children return from afar and that my heart would one day swell with joy (Isaiah 60:4–5).

All through this time I vowed that even if I never saw my son again, I would never stop praying for him. Prayer wasn't the last resort—it was the only thing that I could do for him. The only contact I had with Will was through my Lord Jesus. I believed that my prayers would follow him wherever he went—right into his future. I prayed for healing and reconciliation between us. I also prayed that God would fill Will with supernatural wisdom, that He would surround him with Christian men to be role models and mentors, and that Will would eventually become a Christian. I prayed for his safety, his marriage, his future, his manhood, his career. I prayed that the curse of a broken family would stop with *me*, and that my children would have successful relationships with their spouses. I prayed for all three of my children.

Over the years my MITI high school group morphed into a college and career group, and we prayed our children in and out of college. Some in that group are now grandmothers with another generation to pray for. At Moms In Touch I had a group to pray with during the tragedy of September 2001 when Will was in the Air Force and none of us knew what was happening to our country.

When I separated and divorced, I was so glad to find a group that stood with me and prayed for how my family was being affected. They helped me remember that I didn't need to shoulder the load of this life-altering divorce myself, that God promised to care for me and my children as if He were our husband and father. My weekly MITI meetings were an anchor for me, especially when I would hear the answers to prayers of moms with equally heavy heartaches. Many weeks, the Bible verses that our leader chose seemed to personally fit my situation.

THE WALLS COME DOWN

After four years of praying for my children's hearts and our relationships, Will returned home for a year, and thus began a series of powerful family dramas that broke down the walls, brick by brick.

One night after my mother's sudden death (which was another huge blow for me), my children and I were all sleeping at my parents' house in Seattle. Will woke me in the middle of the night and invited me to the kitchen for a cup of tea.

As tired and sad as I was, I leapt at the chance of an actual conversation with my son. With the snow falling hard outside, we met in the kitchen—I in my flannels and socks and he in his gray sweatpants and T-shirt—and fixed our tea together. Rifling through the freezer, we came upon some cookies my mother had made just days before. We talked until dawn about the divorce and what had happened between us, and slowly, for the first time in years, we heard each other's heart.

In the space of only a few months, one amazing conversation followed another and the lights came on. God showed Will the truth in a way that I could not. Apologies and forgiveness flowed; hearts softened; truth came out satisfying all the questions; patience reigned; and peace and healing, along with miracles that could only be orchestrated by God, finally came to our household.

That year on Valentine's Day morning I opened my front door to find my 6′6″ son standing there with an armful of red roses, a sight I never thought I would see.

Today, Will is in Iraq working again as a firefighter. Our relationship is continuing to heal. He often calls or e-mails to share his life with me, telling me stories about what he is doing, the people he is meeting, and how he feels about everything from the scripture he read that day to the book he just discovered or an opinion he has on politics. Here we are, a mother and a son living on opposite sides of the world. Yet because God has blessed us and healed us, we are closer than we have ever been before.

One evening, not long ago, as I was shopping after work, I chatted with Will on my cell phone for 40 minutes. He was preparing to start his day in a firehouse seven thousand miles away. For so long there had been no communication at all; then what we did say was heavy. Finally, we could just talk and laugh and visit! Things have come full circle—I was chatting in the same store parking lot where Will had ignored me five years earlier. So much has changed, and it has all been brought about by God through prayer.

While we're not a perfect family, today I have a wonderful relationship with all three of my children. All of them are Christians and are growing in the Lord at their own speed and in their own way.

In the last year, each one has written me a letter telling me how grateful they are for the things I have done for them and that I am there for them. I will treasure these letters always. And I also treasure these days, which I appreciate even more fully because I know where we were, and I've seen God's grace in our healing. Yes, my children have returned from afar to the arms of Jesus and to me, and yes, my heart swells with joy.

To all you hurting mothers who have distant and painful relationships with your children, to you who are waiting for them to "come from afar" (whether they are on the other side of the world or under your own roof), I want to encourage you that it's never too late to begin praying for your children and hanging on to God's promises.

I've learned that God is not bound by our mistakes or lack of knowledge. He really is our children's Father—ours, too—and like a good earthly dad, He's eager to give to all of us "abundantly beyond all that we ask or think" (Ephesians 3:20, NASB).

Pray Together

Arise, shine, for your light has come,
>   and the glory of the Lord rises upon you. . . .
Lift up your eyes and look about you:
>   All assemble and come to you;
your sons come from afar,
>   and your daughters are carried on the arm.
Then you will look and be radiant,
>   your heart will throb and swell with joy.

—ISAIAH 60:1, 4–5

Father,
I pray that You would hold on to those of us who are parenting our children alone.
Remind us through Your Word that healing will come in time and that You are the
one who will do it. Melt the darkness in the hearts of our children who are hurting
and protect them from believing any lies. Give us the courage to keep working on
our relationships, the patience to wait for Your perfect timing, and the eyes to see
Your hand. In Jesus' name, amen.

Some trust in chariots and some in horses,
      but we trust in the name of the LORD our God.
They are brought to their knees and fall,
      but we rise up and stand firm.

                                    —PSALM 20:7–8

————

We have not yet learned that a man is more powerful when he is in prayer than when he is in control of the most powerful military weapons we have developed.

                              —BILLY GRAHAM, *Till Armageddon*

Chapter Eighteen
BATTLING SPIRITUAL DECEPTION
by a New Mexico mom

AT 18 YEARS OLD, OUR SON GRANT MOVED TWO THOUSAND MILES AWAY FROM HIS FAMILY AND CHURCH IN NEW MEXICO TO ATTEND HARVARD UNIVERSITY IN CAMBRIDGE, MASSACHUSETTS. GRANT'S IQ WAS OFF THE CHARTS AND HAD A FULL ACADEMIC SCHOLARSHIP; THIS WAS A TERRIFIC OPPORTUNITY FOR HIM. BUT HE WAS SHY AND DIDN'T MAKE FRIENDS IN THE DORM. NOR DID HE FIND A GROUP TO STUDY THE BIBLE WITH HIM.

My husband and I had hoped he'd find a good church, but the few he'd visited near campus all seemed liberal and lifeless, and he wasn't interested in going back. He sounded a bit lonely when we talked to him on the phone. For several months I'd brought these concerns to my college and career Moms In Touch International group, and we'd prayed for our college-aged sons and daughters. We asked for God's protection for Grant's mind and prayed for his faith to grow stronger, and we specifically asked that Grant would not be smothered by intellectualism.

In early November he started a Bible study in his dorm, but no one showed up. Week after week he prepared and put flyers up to invite other students to come, but stopped trying because no one was interested. He also joined a fraternity but was still lonely for spiritual fellowship.

THE INDOCTRINATION PERIOD

During his second semester, Grant was asked by a classmate to discuss spiritual matters over coffee. *Finally*, he thought, *another Christian to share life with*. He couldn't wait for the appointment. When he told us about this new friendship, I thought this must be the answer to our prayers for Christian friends. Finally, God had provided some spiritual companionship for our son.

After getting together several times with this young man, Grant started going to church on Sundays with him and his friends. We were so encouraged to hear he'd found a church, thinking again that our prayers had been answered.

But before long, the young men weren't just inviting him to church or for once-a-week coffee to discuss spiritual issues. They started showing up in his room every single night. Grant had mounds of study and research to do, but he liked having friends, so he welcomed them in and just stayed up later to do his work. The second week of these nightly meetings, they assigned him a "discipler" and began a series of "Bible studies" designed to help him embrace their beliefs and let go of the ones he had grown up with, beliefs they termed "simplistic."

One Sunday night during our once-a-week call, I asked Grant what he was learning in the Bible study. He explained his new take on what the "kingdom" meant. To my knowledge, this "kingdom" definition didn't line up with anything in the Bible about the future kingdom of God with Jesus as the ruler. The teaching at this new Bible study didn't sound right to me, so I talked to my pastor. Two days later, he called me back.

"Jan," he said, "a pastor friend of mine in Massachusetts said that group is known throughout New England and the East coast as a cult. The group targets students on university campuses who are vulnerable, far away from family and friends, and seeking spiritual connections."

MY PANIC BUTTON IS PUSHED

My heart raced when I heard the word *cult*. Grant was just the kind of student the cult was looking for: lonely, vulnerable, away from home, and looking for spiritual fellowship. Now I wasn't just concerned but totally shocked and devastated.

I felt so far away from Grant. I wanted him to know this was dangerous. On our next conversation, I asked, "Grant, this group sounds kind of strange to us. Have you checked this group of guys out? Do you know much about the church they're in?"

"You're just being overprotective!" he replied, offended that we'd question his judgment. "This is a great group of smart guys. They're responsible, moral, and spiritual. And besides, they're Harvard men. Don't worry about me. I can handle this."

The more his dad and I tried to talk to him about what we'd heard about the group, the more resistant he was to hearing our advice. Then a friend gave me the phone number of a couple who had once been sucked into the cult. When I talked to the wife, she told me how horrible and controlling it was and how hard it was for her and her husband to leave. She suggested a few books about the cult for us to read, which I found at a nearby Christian college bookstore. The information I read pushed all my panic buttons. The cult discipler tells you where to live, where to work, how to spend your money, and even whom to marry. In the intermediate stages of discipleship, they demand absolute submission, without question, to someone of higher rank in the church. They have a pyramid power structure headed by their "church evangelist." Once you're in, *you are in.* And it was difficult to get out, like being caught in a spider web. The members are so tightly entrenched in the church that their families have to hire specially trained deprogrammers to get them out.

Yes, my son was bright, but he was being pursued by something controlling and dangerous. I wanted to protect him, but I couldn't, and now he was being encouraged by the cult discipler to make a commitment.

SPIRITUAL "ARMOR"

I was so worried I couldn't sleep. Negative thoughts filled my mind, but when I called Grant again he thought I was overreacting.

"Mom," he said, "I'm trying to seek God in my own way, and I've got to figure this out. I'm in college now. You can't call the youth director and ask him to come pick me up for a gathering. You'll just have to trust God and have faith in me."

That was the tough part—having faith when I wanted to fly up there and shout, "Hold it! Stop!" Then I realized that's exactly what prayer can do. Verses from Ephesians 6 flooded into my mind:

> Put on the full armor of God so that you can take your stand against
> the devil's schemes. For our struggle is not against flesh and blood,
> but against the rulers, against the authorities, against the powers
> of this dark world and against the spiritual forces of evil in the
> heavenly realms. (verses 11–12)

Every week my college and career Moms In Touch group joined in agreement with these prayers for spiritual armor, wisdom and discernment for our son, as well as for wisdom and peace for my husband and me. Oh, how we needed it.

As I read those verses, I knew our family was in a fierce spiritual battle with forces Grant couldn't see or perceive. I prayed earnestly that my son would be totally suited with the armor of God. The imagery that the New Testament presents for this spiritual battle is as follows: the "belt" of spiritual truth, the "breastplate" of righteousness in Jesus Christ, and "ready feet" that come from seeking peace. And added to all this, we prayed that Grant would put on the "shield" of faith in God, the "helmet" of salvation (through Jesus Christ), and the "sword" of God's Holy Spirit, which is Scripture (Ephesians 6:13–18).

The next day, my husband sent Grant a message via e-mail: "Son, don't join anything that you don't know all about." That night our couple's Bible study group, our Moms In Touch members, and dear friends all prayed for Grant—not knowing that this was the exact time the group was asking for his decision about making a commitment. They said he would need to be baptized into their beliefs and church because the baptism he'd had at his home church wouldn't save him. He had to abandon all his former beliefs and fully embrace theirs.

Grant's Choice

Grant called us the next day, "Hey, Mom and Dad, I wanted you to know I told the guys last night I felt God telling me not to pursue their church any further.

"The four men quizzed me over and over, 'How do you know it's God telling you that?' and kept telling me all the benefits of being a part of their church."

"What did you tell them?" I asked.

"I said, 'I just know.' They said that I was arrogant and unteachable, that Jesus recommended leaving my father and mother to join their church, and that it was disobedient to God for me not to, but I stood my ground and stayed firm."

We breathed a huge sigh of relief. Our prayers had been clearly answered.

Whenever I have felt helpless being so far away from my son in the years that followed, God reminded me again, "You stand in the gap by praying *here*, and I'll take care of your son *there*." He has reminded me over and over that He's omnipresent—as present in Massachusetts or New Mexico or anywhere else he may live. He reminded me He's omniscient—that His knowledge includes everything that has existed or will ever exist—and yet He invites me to pray and make known my requests. What a great God we serve!

Pray Together

Therefore put on the full armor of God, so that when the day of evil comes, you may be able to stand your ground, and after you have done everything, to stand. Stand firm then, with the belt of truth buckled around your waist, with the breastplate of righteousness in place, and with your feet fitted with the readiness that comes from the gospel of peace. In addition to all this, take up the shield of faith, with which you can extinguish all the flaming arrows of the evil one. Take the helmet of salvation and the sword of the Spirit, which is the word of God.

—EPHESIANS 6:13–17

Father,
Though my college child is far away, thank You that You are near. Thank You that in prayer there is no distance, and that as I stand in the gap here at the home front, You will work in my son's or daughter's life. Help our college kids be strong in the Lord and the strength of His might, to put on the armor of God and stand against the enemy. Thank You that You are the Victor! In Your almighty name, amen.

They all joined together constantly in prayer, along with the women and Mary the mother of Jesus, and with his brothers.

—ACTS 1:14

The early church didn't have a prayer meeting; the church was a prayer meeting.

—attributed to ARMIN GESSWEIN

CHAPTER NINETEEN
THE LEGACY OF A PRAYING MOM IMPACTS KOREA
by Bok Soon Choi from South Korea

IN 1994, I WAS A BUSY MOTHER WITH A SON, DAUGHTER, AND HUSBAND. YET I ALSO HELPED AT OUR CHURCH AND WAS IN FULL-TIME MINISTRY AS DIRECTOR OF PRECEPT MINISTRIES KOREA. I WAS DOING A LOT OF "GOOD" THINGS. HOWEVER, GOD USED AN ENCOUNTER WITH FERN NICHOLS AT A CHRISTIAN WOMEN LEADERS MEETING IN THE UNITED STATES TO SHOW ME I WAS NOT DOING THE MOST IMPORTANT THING AS A MOM: PRAYING FOR MY CHILDREN. WHILE PRAYING WITH FERN, I REALIZED THAT NO MATTER WHAT ELSE I DID FOR GOD, I WOULD HAVE FAILED IF I DIDN'T PRAY FOR MY TWO CHILDREN, JINJOO AND KYU YOUNG, AS MY MOTHER HAD FAITHFULLY PRAYED FOR ME MANY YEARS BEFORE.

At the end of the meeting that day, Fern and I were prayer partners. When it was Fern's turn to pray, with tears and great earnestness, she prayed first for South Korean moms and children. Then she prayed for North Korean moms and children. I was shocked. I realized I had been so busy with my ministry that I hadn't prayed for my own children with such passion . . . much less for other children. I felt ashamed. Although prayer was taught frequently by Kay Arthur, cofounder of Precept Ministries, I had not made it a priority.

I thought I prayed okay. But I hadn't set a regular schedule to pray for my children and their schools. About four years later, I translated, published, and began using the *Moms In Touch International Booklet.* Although I tried to use the principles in my prayer group, I didn't quite understand them until I went to the 15th anniversary of Moms In Touch in North Carolina (1999). There I learned how to pray according to the Four Steps of Prayer, in one accord, for one hour.

When I returned home, our group began to pray as MITI suggests. At that time, our daughter, Jinjoo, was 14 years old. She was a good kid and attended church services faithfully, but more out of obligation than her own desire. When she went to college, she didn't want to be labeled as a Christian and be set apart from her peers. So she began to drink with them.

"Freedom" from Religion

"I feel greatly burdened when I'm recognized as a pastor's kid at Dad's church," she told us. "I don't have to follow your religion anymore. Now that I am 18, I am free to choose my own. And I am going to leave home."

Those words pierced my heart and scared me to death. She wanted to be free from parents and God. Oh how I cried out to God and prayed for His help alongside the other MITI mothers in our group. After one semester of college, Jinjoo decided to go to L'Abri Fellowship International in England and Switzerland. L'Abri Fellowship International is a place where people search out answers to their spiritual questions, develop a Christian perspective, and live in community.

I was glad she could be away from her partying college friends for a while, but I kept praying for her every week, expecting God to turn her heart and life completely toward Himself. It still has not happened. God seems to say "not yet" to me, and I am waiting for His timing and will—while standing in faith and prayer with my Moms In Touch friends for Jinjoo and their children as well.

In this journey of prayer, God hasn't answered the way I desired. Yet He has changed me from being anxious to being patient, from being critical to accepting of Jinjoo, from seeing only what's happening today to seeing my daughter's entire life span, from holding on to my expectations to yielding to God's, from my desire for her to His desires. That doesn't mean I always succeed at it, but He has been working in my heart as I continue to commit her into His hands alongside my partner MITI moms.

More than anything, I feel so much closer not only to God but also to Jinjoo. We enjoy spending time with each other, and I believe this kind of mother-daughter relationship could not be possible in the midst of her spiritual struggles had I not been praying for her. I also know that God has used Jinjoo to teach me to pray and *love to pray*.

God Breaks a Stronghold

My son, Kyu Young, is a sweet boy, but when he entered eighth grade, he became addicted to computer games. Every day after school he stared at the computer screen, blocking everything else out. He didn't want to interact with us or eat. The only thing he cared about was his five to six hours of computer games a day, and his father and I were unsuccessful in our attempts to stop his obsession.

For a whole semester, my earnest prayer in our weekly Moms In Touch group was "Lord, please stop Kyu Young from playing only computer games!" After that time, I was in England for two months to be with Jinjoo at L'Abri. When I returned to Korea, there had been an amazing change in Kyu Young—he had lost all interest in computer games, not because of my nagging but because God was working in him. Instead of spending hours glued to his computer playing games, he began to study and exercise. As a result, God led him to a good Christian high school, where he came to know God as his Father and Creator by receiving Jesus as his Savior and Lord. With the sincere friends he had there, he diligently sought the Lord and studied hard, and I gathered mothers to pray in a MITI group for that school.

When it was time for Kyu Young to take the entrance exam for college—the SAT test—we prayed and prayed. Though his SAT scores were good, he didn't pass the entrance exam for the outstanding Christian college he wanted to attend. I was disappointed by the result. *Why, God?* I prayed. *I am frustrated. Why didn't You motivate Kyu Young to study harder as I prayed? What do You want from him—and me? I have done what I've known to do as right and yet Your answer is no.*

I kept asking God questions in great disappointment. I felt so miserable that I did not want to meet with anybody and didn't even feel like praying.

A Legacy of Prayer

In my misery, God reminded me of the power of long-range prayers so I would not give up in my intercession for my children. You see, I know the great legacy of a praying parent. My life and ministry are the results of the prayers of my parents, especially my mom's.

When I was a child in South Korea, my parents and the seven of us children lived in the countryside where they farmed. We lived in a small house and all nine slept in the same room to keep warm.

Each morning I heard my mother get up at four o'clock to go to church and pray for her children for at least an hour. As soon as she returned, we could hear her singing praises to God while cooking breakfast. Our father also got up early and sat for an hour praying for each of his children by name and asking for God's help and strength in parenting us.

But as I grew up, I decided my parents were too legalistic. We couldn't use bad words like all the other kids in our village. We were supposed to memorize Scripture, and had to go to church. I wanted to be free from all this "bondage."

So when I turned 19, I was ready to leave home to pursue more education, be a successful woman, and live a life without all the trappings of the Christian culture. The morning I left, my mother urged me to remember God, to go to church on Sundays, and to worship Him.

"Without God, you are nothing, Bok Soon," she said. "I am going to pray for you every day that you will not forget God."

That March, I left my past life behind and went to Seoul, eager to explore big city life. I was willing to study hard even if I had to skip church. One Sunday I decided to go to the library instead of church. But as I was walking there, I heard a church bell ringing.

I tried to ignore the sound, but it kept ringing and ringing in my ears until I remembered my mother saying, "I'm going to pray every day that you will not forget God."

So I turned around and looked for the church. I went in and sat down.

After the service, a lady came up and greeted me warmly. Leading me to the fellowship hall for refreshments, she asked me, "Do you believe in Jesus?"

When I answered yes, she brought out two pictures to show me. One depicted a person sitting on a chair with Jesus at her feet, surrounded by confusion and disorder. The other picture showed Jesus sitting on a chair, with the person at His feet. Order, peace, and balance dominated that picture. "Which describes you better?" she asked.

I could not lie. I knew that the first picture illustrated my life. As we talked, this kind woman gave me assignments of Bible reading and verses to memorize for the next week. As a result, I read Romans and the book of John, over 30 times each, and memorized many verses without understanding them. In October I was listening to a preacher discuss the first chapter of John—about Jesus being the "light of the world" sent by God to die on the cross for our sins.

Suddenly, I was overwhelmed by His love and care. I asked forgiveness for my sins and accepted Christ as my Lord and Savior. All the joy, peace, and love I'd longed for filled my heart. Then everything I'd learned about God from childhood became clear and alive.

As I remembered Mom's and Dad's prayers for me and my siblings every morning, I became so grateful. For all my brothers and sisters, too, our parents' prayers have become a reality in our hearts and lives, and we are all serving Christ.

My life is proof that parents' prayers make a difference in their children's lives. How could I quit praying now even though I was so disappointed about our son's performance and rejection from the college he wanted to attend.

In my misery, God's Holy Spirit spoke a verse to me: "In everything give thanks" (1 Thessalonians 5:18, NASB). At first I couldn't think of anything to thank God *for* about my son's situation. Then He whispered, "*In* everything give thanks!"

I knew I'd better obey God's instructions no matter how bad I felt, so I began to thank God *in* my son's failure. I did it out of obedience by faith, and little by little hope began to spring up in my heart.

GOD'S MYSTERIOUS WAYS

As a family, we began to plan for 2008 and decided that Kyu Young would study one more year to prepare for the college he wanted to attend. As a result, I became a mom who slept only five hours a night and cooked three hot meals a day for our son. I drove him back and forth to the institute where he studied. My husband would say, "What a wonderful mom you are! I respect and appreciate you so much!" Of course, I became a happier wife and mom, and the desire to serve my family grew even more.

Our Seoul Precept Ministries office is near my son's institute, so I moved my home office there and worked on translating some Moms In Touch materials and *The New Inductive Study Bible* by Kay Arthur. Had Kyu Young not failed, I wouldn't have been that productive in 2008.

God has been working among us in mysterious ways: He has drawn us into a closer relationship with Him and to each other. I am learning to worship God as He is, no matter how things turn out, because He is sovereign, loving, and worthy to be worshiped. How sweet is the knowledge that He is there, hears our prayers, and leads us closer to Him. Another way God has worked is that Kyu Young has grown so much spiritually in faith, love, and humility, and our relationship has grown even sweeter. Just the thought of him gives me great pleasure because he reflects the Lord Jesus so clearly.

My dream was for him to become a godly Christian professor in a good college where he can share the gospel with his students. But God has given him dreams to help make the environment better. We know God will work all things together for good for us. After the extra year of study, he took the tests again and applied for three colleges.

SERVING GOD IN KOREA

Today as we await the results of Kyu Young's entrance exams, my desires have become more for what God wants. Kyu Young has decided to major in materials science and engineering to further his desire to help clean up the environment. I pray God will lead my son and daughter into a way that pleases Him and accomplishes true spiritual goals. I ask God to make everything my family does reveal His love and mercy to the world. I also continue to share Moms In Touch with churches all over Korea as well as train the MITI leaders.

Precept Ministries is known as one of the most biblical parachurch organizations and is considered as a great help to Korean Christians. Because my husband, Kyung Sup, and I serve as directors of Precept Ministries Korea and our Precept Press publishes the MITI booklet and materials, one after another, churches have begun to accept MITI as a sound biblical praying ministry. I am so thankful to God for spreading the ministry of Moms In Touch throughout our country via Precept. I want to be a mother whose faithful intercession leaves a legacy of prayer in my children's lives, as my mother did in mine, and I strive to help other moms do the same.

Pray Together

And [Job] said:

> "Naked I came from my mother's womb
>> and naked I will depart.
> The LORD gave, and the LORD has taken away;
>> may the name of the LORD be praised."

—JOB 1:21

Dear Lord Jesus,

Thank You for teaching moms around the world about the importance of prayer. Help moms as they struggle with waiting for answers to prayer. Allow them to see that You have a bigger plan—that by closing one door, You are directing our paths and making Your plan clear. Thank You that You care so much about the character of our children. Thank You that Your best plan for them can include saying "no" to what we think is the best. Thank You that You are a sovereign God. In Your name, amen.

[Jesus said,] "My prayer is not for them alone. I pray also for those who will believe in me through their message."

—JOHN 17:20

———

Prayer is the preparation for every powerful movement of God's Spirit.
—CHERI FULLER, *The One Year Book of Praying Through the Bible*

Chapter Twenty
PRAYING FOR OUR CHILDREN'S FRIENDS

an Indiana mom

As I was driving down the street one June day, I came to a stoplight and noticed two young women wildly waving at me from atop their bicycles. The two girls, my daughter's friends Kelly and Michelle, were home for the summer after completing their first year of college. As I waved back I thought about all the times I have prayed for Emma's friends in our Moms In Touch hour. God has answered those prayers so beautifully over the years!

Kelly and Michelle have been Emma's friends since the fifth grade, the year that my daughter entered public school. They, along with another little girl named Marie, formed a quick foursome. It has been nearly 10 years now, but I remember the many concerns I had for my daughter as she transitioned into a new school situation. Making new friends was high on the priority list. In preparation for the new experience, I prayed she would make good friends and thus be welcomed into her new school environment. Kelly, Michelle, and Marie were the answer to those prayers.

During that first school year, my MITI friends and I prayed for our children not only to *make* good friends but also to *be* a good friend. We focused on James 1:19–20: "Be quick to hear, slow to speak and slow to anger; for the anger of man does not achieve the righteousness of God" (NASB).

The girls were all in the same homeroom that first year. Brown-haired, brown-eyed Emma has always been responsible, organized, and a leader that others look to for counsel and advice. Having three older brothers made her competitive and great at sports. She resisted wearing a dress and insisted keeping her hair in a ponytail. Emma has played tennis since kindergarten and enjoyed being team captain her senior year of high school. I've been blessed to watch her respond with grace and forgiveness even in the competitive world of sports.

Slim Michelle with the dark brown hair was the planner, goal-oriented, and interested in the details. She was competitive when it came to academics, and she loved to swim. Her confidence and independence led the girls on many adventures—she came up with the ideas and then the brainstorming would begin. Michelle would be the one to bring the water balloons to birthday parties.

Marie, bright-eyed and giggly, loved to cook. Like Michelle, Marie was industrious and goal-oriented and came from a family that valued hard work.

Blonde Kelly had flashing blue eyes and braces like many of the girls her age. Highly excitable and eager to spill all her news, she would burst into our home and squeal, "Emma, Emma, you would not believe what just happened!" Kelly loved to paint and draw, and she enjoyed dance troupe.

Despite their differences, the four girls soon became loyal friends with a tight bond, aided by weekend sleepovers, birthday celebrations, and homework sessions together.

WATCHING OUR PRAYERS AT WORK

I always felt these girls were a special combination of personalities. They were not cliquish, like girls who had to have all the same interests or needed to dress alike. I believed God brought them into Emma's life for a reason, and not just to be her friends. At bedtime Emma and I would pray for Kelly, Michelle, and Marie by name. Our prayer was for them to "walk in the light" of God's love, as described in 1 John 1:7: "But if we walk in the light, as he is in the light, we have fellowship with one another, and the blood of Jesus, his Son, purifies us from all sin."

Praying for our children's friends along with our own children has been an ongoing commitment of the moms in our MITI group. We know the importance of our children's peer group, and many times we love these other kids nearly as much as our own. With joy and expectancy in our hearts, we pray and wait to see how God is going to work.

Unfortunately, at the onset of middle school, family life began to deteriorate for Kelly. Divorce and remarriage, as well as the death of a loved one, left her looking for something or someone to hold on to in her life. Emma became that anchor for Kelly and our home a place of refuge as she struggled though years of uncertainty.

At Moms In Touch, when we prayed for our children's friends, these verses fit right into my hopes for the girls: Philippians 1:6, "Being confident of this, that he who began a good work in you will carry it on to completion until the day of Christ Jesus," and Ephesians 2:10 (NASB), "For we are His workmanship, created in Christ Jesus for good works, which God prepared beforehand that we should walk in them." While I had no clear picture of Emma's friends' understanding of Jesus' offer of salvation, I knew God had begun something in their lives. I continued to pray that He would "carry it on to completion."

As the years unfolded through middle school and high school, the girls' friendships continued. There were times of separation when sports, boys, and school commitments created distance in their friendship, but the girls always seemed to be reunited on holidays, birthdays, or special school events. High school graduation seemed to come quickly, and suddenly the girls were off to college. Emma and Michelle attended the same university, Kelly went to another in-state school, and Marie chose to commute to a local college.

COLLEGE DAYS

Psalm 144:12 says, "Then our sons in their youth will be like well-nurtured plants, and our daughters will be like pillars carved to adorn a palace." This is the verse I prayed for Emma, Kelly, Michelle, and Marie as they began college; that God would be shaping them through their experiences into the young women He wanted them to be.

That fall at a prayer conference I heard Fern Nichols tell a story about the growth pattern of a particular species of bamboo. The bamboo doesn't grow for four years, but in the fifth year, it shoots up 80 feet. When she was done speaking she instructed us to turn to someone and pray for a child we knew, that their spiritual life, which might have been dormant, would grow like the bamboo. I immediately thought of Kelly, Michelle, and Marie, these three girls who have been my daughter's friends since fifth grade. I was going to believe God for "80 feet of growth" that year for these girls.

Emma was home for fall break when I returned from the conference, and shortly thereafter Michelle and Kelly dropped by for a visit. Then Marie showed up a bit later. I was so excited to see all the girls together, especially since I had just prayed for them at the conference. Later that evening, after the girls had left, Emma told me she had invited Michelle to attend a small group Bible study at college and she had, indeed, come. She also told me that Kelly had started attending a campus ministry at her college. God answered even before I had prayed!

EIGHTY FEET OF GROWTH

A couple of days later, Emma went back to college. The next day I heard from Marie. Months ago, my husband and I had given her an open invitation to come for dinner, and now she was taking us up on our offer. I was overjoyed that she called, and I wondered if something particular was on her mind.

As I anticipated Marie's visit, I reflected upon how cautious she had become. Gone were the frequent giggles, and I suspected that her industrious nature might be creating some pressure in her life. She was more guarded in her conversations and careful to keep her distance, not wanting to get too close too quickly. I began to pray that she would feel comfortable in our home even though Emma wouldn't be present during her visit.

The next evening, Marie and I enjoyed making shepherd's pie together for dinner. Afterward, as we were clearing the table, I asked her if there was anything specific she wanted to talk about. She told my husband and me about her struggles going to college and working. "Last year, I was so stressed about school and work that I wore myself out," she said. "I know I'm a workaholic, but I feel so responsible for my future. I told this to a friend of mine, and he started talking about the man Job in the Bible, how he suffered through a lot, but he never turned his back on God."

I was curious where the conversation was going, and she continued, "I haven't been going to church, but I did read the Bible a couple times a few years ago. I believe in God. I do. But," she paused, "what exactly does it mean to be a Christian? I feel like I want to start over with God, but I'm not sure how to do it. I asked my friend, and he said all I had to do was believe that Jesus died for my sins. But there must be more to it, because of the way Christians choose to live.

"So," she waited a second before asking the question that had brought her to our home that evening, and said, "how do I become a Christian?"

I could hardly believe my ears! Hadn't I just prayed, not even one week before, for 80 feet of growth for this precious young girl? I thought, *God, this is not at all how I imagined You would work in Marie's life. The moment has come, and*

You're using my husband and me to be the answer to my own prayer for her! At this point I told Marie about the story of the bamboo and how I had prayed for her at the conference.

MEETING JESUS IN THE KITCHEN

As we sat across the kitchen table from her, I told Marie about the many prayers that had been prayed for her over the years and how they had led to this moment. My husband and I told her our experiences of how we learned what it means to have a close relationship with Jesus.

"You know that we love you," we told her. "Well, God loves you even more! But we are separated from God by the sin in our lives, the bad attitudes we have, the questionable choices we make, and even our unbelief."

We opened our Bibles and showed her such key verses as John 3:16: "For God so loved the world that he gave his one and only Son, that whoever believes in him shall not perish but have eternal life." We explained, "Jesus paid the penalty for our sins, bridging the gulf between us and God." After a little more conversation, I gently asked Marie, "Would you like to pray and ask Jesus into your life?"

She said yes, and repeated our prayer, "Dear Lord Jesus, please forgive me of my sins so that I can have a personal relationship with You. Thank You for dying on the cross and rising from the dead three days later so that anyone can join Your family. Thank You that I am now part of Your family. Amen."

I looked up and Marie was beaming as if the moon had penetrated the ceiling and was shining on her face. God's love had penetrated her heart and replaced her worried expression with a radiant smile. I had never seen her so happy before. It was such a memorable moment for each of us. I hugged her and told her how excited I was that she had made this decision for her life. She thanked us for praying with her and wanted to know where to begin as she started reading the Bible again. We offered her a Bible to take with her, which she did, but she was eager to buy her own.

She practically skipped out the door that evening, and she quickly called Emma and Kelly to share her exciting news. They were both overjoyed.

The following weekend Kelly went with Marie to pick out her new Bible.

Years ago, when my husband and I moved our children from private to public school, our desire was to have a home where all their friends would feel accepted and welcome. We wanted our home to be a place where others would see

God's love demonstrated, with the result that someday they would want a home of their own built on that same love.

Ultimately, we wanted them to come to us as Marie did and ask, "What does it mean to be a Christian?" There is no greater impact we moms can make on our children's friends than answering this question. At Moms In Touch, we prayed that God would complete the good work He began (Philippians 1:6) in Emma's friends. That's the promise I stood on, and the promise God kept.

Pray Together

The Lord is not slow in keeping his promise, as some understand slowness. He is patient with you, not wanting anyone to perish, but everyone to come to repentance.

—2 Peter 3:9

———————

Dear heavenly Father,
How amazing it is to see You work in the lives of our children and their friends. Please, Lord God, in Your patience and love, bring the young people to You. Open their eyes to truth and surround them with Christians who will share with them Your love and plan for their lives. In Jesus' loving name, amen.

Before they call I will answer;
 while they are still speaking I will hear.

—Isaiah 65:24

———

Prayer is talking with God and telling him you love him, conversing with God about all the things that are important in life, both large and small, and being assured that he is listening.

—C. Neil Strait, quoted in
Prayer: Webster's Quotations, Facts, and Phrases

Chapter Twenty-One
HELP FOR A CHILD WHO SCORED IN THE "1 PERCENTILE"
by an Oregon mom

*M*OMS IN TOUCH INTERNATIONAL PRAYER TIME WAS JUST BEGINNING IN OUR SOUTHERN OREGON COMMUNITY. WE HAD FORMED A NEW GROUP IN THE FIRST WEEK OF SEPTEMBER 1998. MEETING WITH EXCITEMENT, FOUR WOMEN HUDDLED AROUND A RED CHROME KITCHEN TABLE IN THE HOME OF ONE OF OUR MOMS. WE WERE READY TO GIVE GOD THE CHALLENGES THAT WOULD FACE OUR CHILDREN IN THE UPCOMING SCHOOL YEAR.

One morning early in March, I arrived at the meeting upset and burdened. When we got to the intercession time of sharing our children's greatest needs, I told the other moms about a test result I'd just received from my third grader, Carol, who was now in a new school. On the standardized test, Carol had scored well in most subjects but was low in comprehension. In fact, my daughter scored in the *1 percentile.* Although she was a fast reader (about 130 words per minute), the testing showed that Carol *did not comprehend anything* she was reading.

"How could this be? She did so well in first and second grade," her dad and I questioned. She always scored 100 percent on her spelling tests. Examiners told us that Carol had developed a sharp mind for memorization. Until third grade, she had been able to keep up with schoolwork by the pure determination to memorize. Now that schoolwork was becoming more complex, she no longer could slip by on this talent alone.

My heart broke when I thought about how bleak the future could be for a little girl who couldn't understand the words on a page. From what the educators told us, it seemed she might not have the skills to make it to college or achieve her dreams. So besides asking for a miracle, I asked my friends to pray that I could find peace during the uncertain road ahead.

ANXIETY AND FEAR

School officials began to pay special attention to Carol's learning disability, but the result was not what we expected. Carol began to experience severe anxiety and fear. This was her first year at a new school, and she didn't want to be seen as different by the other children. Most of all, she did not want anyone to know she needed help with her reading. Nonetheless, three times a week she was called out during class to spend time with the special-education teacher.

At the end of each session, the teacher would bring her back into class while all eyes were watching. Kids can be cruel and began reacting to the embarrassment Carol was showing. As these reactions escalated, Carol's anxiety did also. Her bowels became uncontrollable, and she begged me to let her stay home from school. She would cry when separated from her dad and me because we were the only security she had, the only people with whom she felt safe.

Each week as we gathered to pray I shared about Carol's progress and setbacks. Though thanksgivings were in order for the progress Carol was making in her reading comprehension, help was needed for the decline in her self-esteem—and for the discouragement and anxiety I often felt. To have these moms put their arms around me and support me through this trial was a lifeline from God.

A PRAYER FOR BOLDNESS

In the middle of March, I cried out to God, "Father, you did not give Carol a spirit of timidity, but a spirit of power, of love and of self-discipline." I prayed using 2 Timothy 1:7, and inserting Carol's name. The other moms prayed along that God would deliver her from all her fears and give her courage, understanding, and perseverance. And week after week, the moms prayed with me about her attitude toward school. The problems mounted, but each week as we met we found new areas in which to specifically ask God to intervene.

It was nearing the end of the school year, and we were getting ready to break from our MITI group for the summer. We had seen God answer many requests and were encouraged as another year ended. We would not formally meet again until the following fall, but these faithful women committed to pray for my daughter over the break. I had enrolled her into a summer program so she wouldn't lose the progress that had been made.

After school dismissed and vacation time started, I began noticing almost immediately a complete difference in Carol's demeanor. She was happy again, and the trouble with her bowels had subsided. But this was to be short-lived. As fall quickly approached, all fear and anxiety returned.

No Visible Progress

School was in session once again, and two more moms joined our MITI group. As we all began to share about the obstacles for the upcoming year, I felt the heavy burden I had for Carol. Little or no academic progress had been made. Carol's attitude about school was worse than ever, and her bowel trouble returned. The outward signs were not positive; however, we all knew that God was at work in Carol, even though we could not see it.

One year after we found out about the reading comprehension deficit, my husband and I were once again called to a conference with Carol's teacher; this time we were informed she was having difficulty in math. Our concerns were growing, and now there was a new problem to deal with. Yet God gave us a peace and calm about this new discovery.

When Carol was in fifth grade, it was time for her to be retested. To reassure Carol, the test proctors let me sit in a nearby room while the testing took place. I could talk to her between breaks and praise her for not giving up. The tests were all packaged up and sent to the school district for scoring.

Two weeks later the scores were in. Carol had improved to 50 percent comprehension. We were thrilled. She was now on her way to higher comprehension and understanding. My husband and I were confident that schoolwork would now start to make sense to Carol; however, she still had the wounds of embarrassment to deal with.

At the next Moms In Touch meeting, as we gathered once again around that red chrome kitchen table, our prayers were focused on gratitude and thanksgiving for what God had done and the progress Carol had made. Then in the intercession time, our petitions turned to healing for Carol's body because the bowel problems were a source of shame and embarrassment to her. Confident that God would continue to work in Carol's life, I was able stop worrying about this emotional burden and wait for God to act.

High school days eventually came, and we enrolled Carol in a Christian school. By God's grace, she was able to enjoy the years there without any anxiety or physical issues. Her comprehension had surpassed what many educators thought was possible. When she took a standardized test in her junior year, she scored 100 percent on reading comprehension.

Through the persistent prayers of faithful moms and a lot of years of extra work at home to help our daughter, we were able to watch her do amazingly well in high school. Not only had her language and math skills improved, but Carol had a real understanding of the grace of God in her life, more so than most young people her age.

FEAR REPLACED BY COURAGE

This young woman, who had once been gripped by fear, did fundraising for a year so she could go on a missions trip. Once afraid to go anywhere without her parents, she left on a journey to Ireland with other students and chaperones the summer before her junior year. Her sense of adventure is now so evident to everyone who knows her that they'd never imagine she'd been so timid and afraid.

Today Carol is in her first year of college and achieved a 4.0 for the first semester. She is strongly rooted in the love of God and shines among her peers in her commitment to Him. When checking her Facebook page on the computer recently, I saw this statement posted: "Oh, I just got my paper back from my writing professor, and I got an A. Woot! I'm so glad!"

My daughter isn't just surviving her college years, but thriving and succeeding in her studies. The young girl who once scored in the 1 percentile in reading comprehension and struggled in math has exceeded everyone's expectations, including her own.

Pray Together

[I pray that you,] being rooted and grounded in love, may be able to comprehend with all the saints what is the breadth and length and height and depth, and to know the love of Christ which surpasses knowledge.

—Ephesians 3:17–19 (nasb)

———————

All-wise God,

We pray for our kids who have trouble learning. We ask that You would help them understand and comprehend what they study. Heal their minds so they can not only do well in school but also read and understand Your Word, the Bible. Protect them from being ridiculed for being different and deliver them from all their fears. Draw their moms close to Your heart so they will know that nothing is impossible with You! In Christ's name, amen.

Through you we push back our enemies;
   through your name we trample our foes.

                        —Psalm 44:5

––––––––––

When we bring God's Word into our prayers, it infuses vitality . . . it gives [our]
prayers life . . . [we] are better able to frame [our] thoughts around God's thoughts;
[our] will around God's will; [our] desires around His.
               —Joni Eareckson Tada, "Praying God's Word,"
                        Joni and Friends radio transcript

CHAPTER TWENTY-TWO
THE VALLEY OF ADDICTION
by an Illinois mom and her daughter, Shannon

SHANNON'S STORY:

THE FIFTH GRADE POPULAR GIRLS WERE WHISPERING TOGETHER AT LUNCH LIKE THEY DID EVERY DAY. I WAS SITTING BY MYSELF AT THE SAME TABLE, A FEW SEATS DOWN, READING A BOOK. ONE OF THE GIRLS SAID, "WHOEVER LIKES SHANNON, RAISE YOUR HAND." NO ONE RAISED HER HAND. THEY GIGGLED AND GLARED MOCKINGLY AT ME. "WHOEVER THINKS SHANNON IS PRETTY, RAISE YOUR HAND." NO HANDS. "WHOEVER THINKS SHANNON IS WEIRD, RAISE YOUR HAND." THEY ALL EAGERLY RAISED THEIR HANDS AT THAT ONE.

Every day girls would "accidentally" bump into my desk as they walked by, sometimes pushing me down. Sometimes they would tell a boy to pretend to like me, get my hopes up that somebody liked me, and then he would announce to the entire playground that it was a joke and that no one could ever like Shannon.

Rejection came at me from all directions at school, except from teachers who often complimented me on how smart I was. But I just wanted to hide behind my hair, be invisible, or be someone completely different, someone that everyone liked. Fear of rejection and the ridiculously strong desire to be liked by everyone grew and grew until they were the sole components in every action I took.

I started my addiction to self-harm at age eight and, like any addiction, it progressed over time. In second or third grade when I got upset, I would bang my head against the wall or hurt myself with a pencil or sometimes just fall off the monkey bars or stub my toe on purpose.

DEEP DEPRESSION

My depression was noticeable in sixth grade. I was sent to therapy. The therapist sexually abused me. I blamed myself and God.

In middle school I discovered that cutting myself brought more instant gratification. Over time, the cuts got deeper; there would be more, on different parts of my body, and from all different types of tools. Burning was convenient for school if I wanted to hurt myself . . . all I needed was a lighter or an eraser to rub against my skin.

Sometimes the injuring was to punish myself for not being good enough; sometimes it represented the aggression I wanted to take out on others; sometimes I wanted to stop panic attacks; sometimes I just wanted the scars. I wore my scars like medals. I was proud of them and for a long time I believed that they defined who I was.

In middle school I continued with self-harm, developed an eating disorder, and was seeking love in all the wrong places. My struggle with drugs and alcohol began at age 11. Throughout middle school I messed around with pot, alcohol, acid, pills, cocaine, speed, and boys.

Yet even though I had one life as an addict, my other life was that of a good student who loved her family and faithfully went to church and youth group. I believed in God, but I was convinced that His salvation could not apply to me.

In the winter of my freshman year, two positive things happened: (1) My parents sent me to a series of outpatient programs to address my various disorders, and (2) I joined a Christian drama program, which gave me a new group of friends. My new friends encouraged me and made me question my shady behavior and distorted thinking. But I was unable to grasp the help that was being offered. And somehow throughout all of this, my drug life remained undetected by all the doctors, therapists, and family members.

In June of 2007, I was admitted into a drug rehab program. That was an answer to my mom's prayer even though at the time it seemed like a curse to me. Getting sober was what made me look at myself and my relationship with God. It made me realize I did want a relationship with Jesus Christ. And because of that, I have accepted my identity as a precious daughter of Christ, regardless of my actions or past decisions. Through all this my mom continued to pray.

Here is her story.

MOM'S STORY

My daughter, Shannon, had a passion for Jesus and prayer from a young age. We would pray on the way to school every day—it was only a few minutes' ride, but that helped refocus the day after the rush-rush of getting to school on time.

Her prayers were so genuine and down to earth: "Jesus, please be with Brandon today. He's been so mean lately." "Please help the secretary not yell at any kids today." "Remind that boy on the bike to look both ways." She also kept her own prayer journals in first and second grade, and prayed for all of her classmates.

Shannon was born independent. When I left her at Sunday school at age two, she said, "Bye, Mommy. You can go now." Though she was petite, her long, straight blonde hair was often in braids and out of her way—she was not a frilly girl. Her best friend in kindergarten was a neighbor boy, until he learned it wasn't cool to be friends with a girl.

Shannon was verbally advanced and could converse with anyone. However, she had trouble with her peers—as early as first grade she complained that no one liked her. By third grade she frequently reported that everyone made fun of her, though her teachers said she was doing well and they couldn't see that she was having any particular problems with her peers. In fifth grade Sunday school, she didn't feel like she fit in so she started sneaking out of class to be by herself. Sixth grade Sunday school was better—we went to a smaller church, which Shannon enjoyed very much because the youth group was small and had no "in crowd."

PRAYER THAT EXPOSES

Before my children were school age, I heard about MITI on a Focus on the Family radio broadcast. It brought me such peace to know I could pray for my children while they were at school. When Shannon entered first grade and my neighbor told me she was leading an MITI group for the elementary school, I think I shocked her by my immediate and enthusiastic commitment!

Within the next several years I moved from merely attending the group to leading it and helping to field questions about what we did. I eagerly read all the material and attended every MITI event offered. God was preparing me to be a committed prayer warrior.

However, as Shannon entered middle school, I became more and more aware that something wasn't right. She wanted friends but didn't have any; she was growing overly sensitive about herself. When she fell into depression in sixth grade, we sought counseling for her. I would like to report that with counseling she immediately improved, but that was not the case. Little did I know it would greatly exacerbate the problems.

My lifeline was MITI, and I was relieved there was a group for Shannon's middle school. I couldn't wait to start praying with them, especially as I could get no lock on what was going on in my daughter's life. However, when I got there I was disappointed to find only one other woman—where was this group that was going to help me? Though there were just two of us, I learned that "where two or three have gathered in My name, I am there in their midst" (Matthew 18:20, NASB).

I was expecting some trials as Shannon moved into adolescence but certain behaviors she developed seemed over the top. She was growing attracted to dark things—books and music I didn't approve of, violent crime shows, and a mild interest in Goth. She was too self-conscious to draw attention to herself, so black eyeliner was as far as her appearance changed. After 9/11, I saw more withdrawal and sadness. She often seemed anxious and wanted to take on the world's problems. She retreated to TV, movies, and reading—lots of solitary pastimes.

Shannon maintained good grades and a good relationship with us, but still rarely had friends. At home she had plenty of backbone; at school she became the girl who was picked on or used. When she did hang out with other girls, afterward all she could talk about was what was wrong with them. That was something we continually saw in her—she was so judgmental and critical of everyone that no one was good enough to be her friend. It seemed she would rather be alone than be with friends she didn't think were perfect. I'd try to help her explore her own feelings, but she'd usually turn the question around. "Mom, all they want to talk about is boys."

We realized later that Shannon's judgmental attitude was probably due to how overly critical she was of herself. She spent a lot of time overanalyzing all of her own faults and weaknesses. Her negative view of herself escalated into more anxiety and depression. Then we started noticing signs of self-harm, which we had missed before. She told a new counselor she was thinking of suicide and had tried to ingest ant poison.

At our Moms In Touch time, we prayed big prayers about huge concerns that only God could handle—prayers that Shannon would find friends who would be good influences on her, prayers for protection from all sorts of things including the media (movies, books, TV, music), prayers that she wouldn't be "tempted beyond what [she could] bear" (1 Corinthians 10:13), and prayers about her inclination to self-injury. We prayed little prayers, too, for everyday life—choices about clothes, makeup, hygiene, tests, and projects.

PRAYING IN ALL THE RIGHT PLACES

Every week we prayed for me, too—what I should or should not do, that my husband and I would find the correct treatment for Shannon and receive godly guidance and intervention from other adults. We prayed for physical and spiritual protection for our whole family, that things we needed to know would be known, and that we would catch Shannon if she were doing something wrong.

It was during Shannon's eighth-grade year that I heard a mom give a moving testimony of her own daughter's battle with self-injury at the Moms In Touch Anniversary Celebration in Dallas. The girls' stories were so similar, and it encouraged me to hear how God was working in another family with a lot of the same concerns. We were invited to pray with others near us. I turned around to pray with a stranger, and, because of what we'd just heard, I felt free to open up about all I was dealing with. We prayed for protection and for God to reveal the root of Shannon's depression and lead us to the right treatment for her. We thanked God together that she hadn't been successful in her suicide attempt.

That prayer gave me a new freedom to more boldly and transparently share my prayer requests with other moms. In our MITI group back home, when new moms came and I felt insecure, I reinforced the confidentiality policy that "what is prayed in the group, stays in the group." When I was transparent, the other women felt free to be open as well. There is a lot of power in that kind of safety.

PRAYER THAT ENLIGHTENS

Shannon's junior year proved to be the turning point. A local rehab program sponsored a parent education seminar at the high school. My Moms In Touch group prayed that whatever parents needed to be there would be, and that the seminar would serve God's purposes. I attended, believing that Shannon's issues weren't drug related, but thinking the information would help me identify drug use in my kids, or their friends, in the future. The evening was filled with eye-opening information, including testimonies from kids in the program who talked about the many ways they hid their behavior. It turned out I was praying for myself and didn't even know it!

The following summer my husband and I became aware of Shannon's undiagnosed drug addiction. She had fooled not only us, but many "expert" psychiatrists and counselors. It angered me that the *professionals* hadn't caught Shannon's drug problem. But, thankfully, you can't hide anything from God, nor can you stop Him from working in your heart.

Which is exactly what He did. Shannon came to the point where her heart softened enough to consider making the necessary changes. There weren't a lot of outward manifestations; all along Shannon had looked okay on the outside. That was part of the problem. But when she began to tell the truth about her drug lifestyle to us and to all her counselors, it was obvious that the freedom she felt was a big relief. We all enrolled in a family drug rehab program, and my husband and I found support from other families going through the same thing. This program emphasized "obeying the rules," not just pretending to; choosing friends; dealing with social discomfort and body image; and many more issues.

My husband and I learned to take back the God-given leadership in our family, including imposing the strict limits Shannon needed, especially while coming off the drugs. We finally began to understand the harsh reality of being an addict and what led Shannon to this lifestyle in the first place. The whole story of her depression, anxiety, sexual assault, self-harm, eating disorder, and drug addiction came out, and all aspects of her distorted thinking and negative coping skills began to be addressed. Yes, I was grieving with the new information, but I'd gone through so much with her already that my most powerful emotion was thankfulness that the light was now on.

Shannon resisted some of the difficulties of the strict rehab program, but she did it! Even after she turned 18 and could have discharged herself and left home, she chose to complete the program and work toward sobriety. She returned to regular Bible study and prayer, sang with the church worship team, and worked at a Christian preschool.

My MITI friends continued to pray that Shannon would be led by people who believed in prayer, in the power of God, and in the important role of parents. Everywhere we turned, God provided the godly guidance we'd all been praying for. Shannon became involved in a Celebrate Recovery ministry. Our family visited a church that was starting a sermon series on 12-step programs from a

Christian perspective. Shannon rushed to talk to the pastor after one Sunday service, so excited to share that she was "one week sober!" She was later baptized there by the same pastor.

Prayer That Sustains

This past summer I listened to my daughter tell her story at a Celebrate Recovery meeting. She stood before 40 people, nervous and excited. Her long, golden blonde hair and bangs shone, and her face radiated health and confidence. You can imagine the flood of tears when I heard her say that she knew it was her mom's prayers that kept her alive, and that it was her mom who showed her what faith is.

It's not over yet. We are still having to make some tough decisions on Shannon's behalf, but she's part of that decision-making process, and she is a remarkable woman who continues to grow in her faith. She has successes and failures, but she continues to see her counselor and attend rehab meetings, and she shares her prayer requests with her mom!

I knew all along, throughout this whole journey, that God personally called me into the MITI ministry, and He sent others to encourage and lead me. I have been so blessed to see God's miracles in my family, and so grateful to be taught to pray all the time about everything. Because of what we've been through, I'm now involved with many hurting families, and I love and pray regularly for many addicted teens. Other moms of addicts I know are surprised at how calm I am. It's only because I know this is *all* in God's control and in His timing. I've been able to encourage them not to give up or ever stop praying. I love sharing that being involved in the prayer ministry of Moms In Touch, long before I knew how much my family needed it, was the main thing that gave me hope during dark and scary times.

Shannon is attending community college now and loves her classes. It is a miracle she is alive and that she still has many functioning brain cells! She's working toward a degree in early childhood education; she already has a great intuition for zeroing in on kids who need some special attention. She's using her leadership gifts to organize service projects and is involved in helping other kids who struggle with addictions.

Shannon also continues to participate with Celebrate Recovery, and this is her testimony: "I know now that Jesus' scars on His hands and feet cover all of mine."

Pray Together

[Jehoshaphat said,] "We have no power to face this vast army that is attacking us. We do not know what to do, but our eyes are upon you." . . .

[God's prophet answered,] "Do not be afraid or discouraged because of this vast army. For the battle is not yours, but God's."

—2 Chronicles 20:12, 15

———————

Dear Lord Jesus,
So many times we moms don't know what to do when we see our children suffering so intensely. Give us the faith to trust in Your strength and not rely on our own. We praise You that You are working all things together for good for our children. Give us Your peace and remind us every single day that You hold us and our children in the palm of Your hand. In Your faithful name, amen.

[Jesus said,] "If you then, being evil, know how to give good gifts to your children, how much more will your heavenly Father give the Holy Spirit to those who ask Him?"

—Luke 11:13 (NASB)

———————

Next to the wonder of seeing my Savior will be, I think, the wonder that I made so little use of the power of prayer.

—*attributed to* D. L. Moody

Chapter Twenty-Three
From Prison to Peace

by Regina Rives, a mom who learned to pray in a Texas prison

As I LAY ON MY BUNK, I GAZED AT THE CEILING TRYING TO FIGURE OUT HOW MY LIFE HAD COME TO THIS. *HOW DID I END UP IN PRISON?* I ASKED MYSELF. *GOD, WHY? WHY WOULD YOU ALLOW ME TO COME HERE? HOW COULD YOU TAKE ME AWAY FROM MY CHILDREN?*

I wondered what they were doing right then. My snuggly two-year-old Landen didn't understand. He rarely cried when I was with him; would he cry tonight for his mommy? Would Holly's dad understand all the changes she's going through as a young teen? Physically, my blonde-haired, blue-eyed daughter had matured early, but she was still innocent and needed her mom. *God, I feel so awful that I'm not there to help her through this time.*

The tears were forming. I tried to hold them back, but I couldn't. My chest ached as I lay there grieving as if I would never see my children again. I could no longer hear their voices, touch them, smell them. This was agony. And it was just the beginning.

That was March 8, 2007, the day I arrived at a federal prison camp in Texas. After having lunch, my husband, Chris, and I made the three-hour drive that sunny morning. I knew this was hard enough on my husband, and I didn't want to make it worse for him. I could see the worry in his blue eyes as we drove along the two-lane Texas roads. He always took care of us with such kindness and gentleness, but for the first time I was going through something he could do nothing about.

"This is the hardest thing I've ever done, honey," he told me. When we arrived at the prison camp and said a quick good-bye, I tried to smile as he drove away. I wanted to seem brave but inside my heart was shattering. How could I go through the days and weeks without my strong yet tenderhearted husband?

As I took a first glance around the prison, I remember thinking, *This doesn't look so bad. I can do this.*

But moments later, as I paced back and forth in the holding cell, my thoughts raced. I was so nervous, I couldn't keep still. Fear was creeping in, taking over any control I once had.

God, please help me through this, I thought. That's when I met Sherry, who also had just arrived. There was something special about Sherry, something comforting about her presence. Her words were encouraging, and I suddenly felt relaxed with her there.

I clung to Sherry when we entered the dorm, as if I had known her my whole life. *What are the odds of us bunking together?* Looking out at the crowded unit, I thought, *It's a wonder they have a bed for me at all with this many women.*

After I found Room 63, I decided I'd go climb on my bunk, not speak to anyone, and just keep to myself. *That's what you're supposed to do in prison,* I told myself. I was exhausted. *If only I could get a little sleep,* I remember thinking. But as I lay there that night on the hard bed, it seemed the tears would never end. Sleep wouldn't come. I pleaded with God, "Lord, I thought I could be strong. I thought I could do this on my own, but I can't."

"Where are You, God?" I asked. "Please wrap me in Your arms and bring me peace." That was the last thing I remember saying late into the night. The next morning I awoke with a deep weight of grief on my chest that wouldn't go away. I lay there as the women hurried to get ready for breakfast, their voices reverberating across the steel beams and concrete floors. I could not believe the noise!

A FAMILY TORN APART

My thoughts suddenly turned to my children. The pain in my chest became unbearable and my eyes became blurred as tears rolled down my face. I turned and faced the wall, pulled the blanket over my head, and began to sob. I couldn't hold back; it hurt too much. I wanted my kids and my husband. Our family had been torn apart. *If I could just hear their voices.* I longed to hear Holly's laughter as she told a joke or was having fun with her friends. Now she was with her father, my former high-school sweetheart. Precious little brown-eyed Landen—I could picture him toddling around in his diaper, brightening up every place he went. Landen also was placed in the home of his biological father, even though he had never lived with him. We partied together but never had a more permanent relationship. Shortly after I found out I was pregnant, he was sent to prison and had never established contact with or provided for his child.

As time went on, after I stopped doing drugs because of my pregnancy with Landen, I thought, *Thank goodness I survived that and didn't kill myself or get arrested.* I was grateful I was away from the drug dealers and had cleaned up my life. I was so thankful to be with Chris, a kind, gentle man who knew all about my past but loved me anyway. We were attending church together and were starting a new life with my children.

But one day I was putting away groceries, and two agents from the Drug Enforcement Agency knocked on my door. Someone had turned me in to get off his own drug charges. The agents had been watching me, and now, three years after my drug involvement, I was being indicted.

When they led me away in handcuffs, my husband was left at home with just the dogs—our mother dachshund and her new puppies. *If only there had been a way for Landen to stay with Chris, because that's who he looks to as "Daddy." Then at least they'd be together,* I thought. Yet I knew his biological dad wouldn't agree to that.

"What have I done to my family?" I said between sobs. "Were drugs and money worth putting them through this? The children don't deserve to have their mommy taken away and their lives turned upside down."

"God, please help me!" I cried out. "Please make it stop hurting."

"Regina," I heard someone say. Turning my head, I saw it was Sherry. "Do you want to go to lunch with me?" she asked.

I got up, wiped my face, and slipped on my shoes. As we gathered downstairs in the dining hall with all the women, I noticed a bulletin announcing religious services. *Wow,* I thought, *church, Bible study, and spiritual healing classes.* They had a full schedule.

A GLIMPSE OF HOPE

That's when I saw it: *Moms In Touch International.* The sign said, "Come pray for your children, their schools, their caregivers, etc., on Wednesday nights." *I could go to that,* I told myself, *but the meeting is days from now.* The tears were welling up again. *Oh no,* I thought. *Not now, not here in front of everybody.* My eyes began to burn; a lump had formed in my throat.

"I'll be back," I told Sherry, as I made my way to the restroom. I locked the door and buried my face in my hands. "God, please help me," I pleaded. "Where are You? My children need me. What am I doing here?"

I felt as though the Lord had abandoned me. It was a feeling I was growing accustomed to. If my mom and dad did not want me as a little child, why would God? Why would He want to help someone as broken and sinful as I am? My past had finally caught up with me. For so many years, I'd turned my back on the Lord. I'd denied Him over and over. Now I thought He was denying me. "Please, God, I cannot do this alone. I need You," I begged.

"Regina, you in here?" It was Sherry.

"Yeah, just a second."

"It's time for chow," she yelled. I wiped my tears and cleaned my face the best I could, but there was no doubt that I was hurting.

Some women offered a smile, some a kind word. I even heard a joke or two, but there was no laughter in me. I sat picking at my food.

"How about some fresh air?" Sherry asked. *I could use a little fresh air,* I thought. *Wow, what a big place this is,* I thought as I glanced around the prison yard. I looked at the women along the track and throughout the compound. *How can they smile and laugh as if they were happy?*

Surely many of them were mothers too. Were their babies at home missing them? Were their husbands worried if they were okay? How could they possibly find joy in this place? How could they not feel guilty for their laughter? What a contrast to how I felt: Only sorrow filled my body and mind. Not one ounce of joy was left in me. All I could think about was the pain I felt. My heart ached for my family, my home, my church, and my life.

Finally, it was Wednesday—a chance to tell someone how I missed my children. Could they help me? What exactly was Moms In Touch anyway? I made my way toward the chapel. As I approached the door, I saw the sign "Moms In Touch will be held here tonight." As I stepped in, I was greeted by a room of friendly faces.

"Hi, I'm May, a volunteer with Moms In Touch. Have you been here before?" she asked.

"No, I just got here a few days ago," I replied as my eyes began to burn.

"Grab a seat and let me introduce you and tell you a little about Moms In

Touch," she explained.

As she talked I suddenly became overwhelmed. *Pray out loud?* I thought, *I've never done that before. What will I say?*

As the meeting went on, it seemed I was the only one in the room who hadn't prayed. I fell silent, and then I felt a warm hand on mine, as if to say, "It's okay, we're here for you."

"Lord," I began. "I give Holly and Landen to you. Please protect them and comfort them." My eyes began to burn, my voice began to crack, and the tears cascaded down my face. "It hurts," I sobbed. "It hurts so bad." All the pain I'd been feeling poured out as I cried uncontrollably. The other women, each grabbing hands, began to pray for me.

As they prayed for my children and my husband, I felt so much comfort. For the first time I sensed the presence of the Lord in that prison. God placed these words in my heart that night: "I can do all things through Him who strengthens me" (Philippians 4:13, NASB). No matter what happened, I would hold on to that verse as a reminder that God was in control and He would bring me through this.

As the hour came to an end, I was approached by two girls who told me their stories, their hurts, and how they had felt the same way in the beginning. *So I know I am not the only one who cries, who hurts,* I thought. As I looked around at each person in that room, I could sense peace in them. So many stories, so much suffering—yet they were at peace. *That's a peace that only God can bring,* I thought. *That is a peace I want.*

CAN THE HURT GO AWAY?

As we walked back to the dorm that night, I listened to the women's stories and their laughter. I walked watching, observing. I told God, "I want the hurt to go away; I want to have peace also." Then He reminded me again: "I can do all things through Him who strengthens me" (Philippians 4:13, NASB).

That night I borrowed a Bible from my roommate. As I turned the pages I came to Psalm 34:18: "The LORD is close to the brokenhearted and saves those who are crushed in spirit."

As I read those words, it was as if God were telling me, "I'm here with you. I will never leave you. We will get through this together." I found so much comfort in His words.

Weeks passed. Each day became a little easier. I never stopped grieving for my children, but it didn't hurt as much. I still struggled with fear and anxiety. I worried that the children missed me and would soon forget who I was. Landen was so young. Would he begin to call someone else "Mommy"? And Holly . . . she must feel lost without her mother. I would pray, "God, tell my babies I love them. Tell them Mommy misses them." When I got to speak to my husband on the phone, I cried. I wanted so much to see my kids and hug them.

Each week I met with Moms In Touch, I began to see changes in myself and my family. I began to realize the importance of prayer and how it changes our lives. Looking back I saw that when I first went to prison, I was angry at God and tried to convince Him I didn't belong there. When I stopped blaming Him, I realized it was not God's fault. *It was mine.* He wasn't punishing me and my family. As I accepted the responsibility and consequences of my wrong choices, I found that God would be there for me and walk with me through the months of incarceration.

There were times I prayed selfishly, asking God to put it on the judge's heart to give me an immediate release. Sometimes I allowed the hurt and the anger to keep me from seeing what it was God had planned for me. But when I continued to read my Bible, I found that God would often use certain verses to reveal Himself to me. I also discovered the power Scripture had when used in prayer.

GROWING IN GOD'S WORD

I learned so much from the women in my Moms In Touch group. The New Testament says, "Where two or three come together in my name, there am I with them" (Matthew 18:20). I believe this with my whole heart. I went into this group with a selfish heart, wanting my pain to end, wanting my own children to be protected. What I learned was something very different. These women genuinely cared for one another and each other's children. When we prayed, it was for one another, *never just one's self* or just one's own kids. Although I never had the chance to meet their kids, I feel I will always have a bond with them through prayer.

I began to believe that God hears our prayers and that it pleases Him to answer them, like our prayers for my two-year-old son who'd been sent to live with a father he didn't know. Though it seemed impossible—through the continued prayers of our MITI group and the help of my grandmother—Landen's father and my husband were able to work out joint custody, so Landen could be with my husband on the weekends.

When I went into the federal prison camp, my daughter was angry and at times refused to visit me. She carried a lot of shame because her mom was in prison. She began to isolate herself from family and friends. I heard reports that her grades were slipping and her conduct at school was poor. She became disrespectful with her teachers and often ended up in detention. She was out of control.

After months of praying and asking God to help her, I began to see changes in my daughter. She began to accept my phone calls. Instead of yelling, she would tell me she missed me and couldn't wait for me to come home. She often talked about going shopping together and how she wanted me to help her decorate her room. Her relationship with her father also improved, as did her grades and behavior at school. God had answered my prayers.

RELEASING FEAR AND CONTROL

I had always been the type of woman to worry about and fear what I could not control. Being in prison left me continually worrying about my children, because I no longer had the ability to care for them or protect them. Though it kept me from experiencing the peace and joy God had for me, worrying gave me the feeling that I had some control. But I discovered in our Moms In Touch group that God loves my children even more than I do, and He will take care of them. I gained true friends, one of whom I'm still in contact with today. I realized that it's not all about me and what I'm going through; God wants me to pray for others and care about them. I learned that I can trust in His Word that hardships and trials are meant to build our faith and teach us spiritual maturity. And most important, I learned to pray.

One night while praying I gave my children over to God. *Completely!* I gave back what already belonged to Him. I realized that my children are His, and I am blessed to be their mother. The spirit of fear and worry lifted, and peace descended upon me.

At one of our meetings, we read, "Cast all your cares upon Him, for He cares for you" (1 Peter 5:7 NASB). I discovered that means not *some* of our cares and burdens, but *all*. Especially our children. And when we come together in prayer with other moms and lay all our burdens before Him, I experience His promised rest. That is why I believe Moms In Touch is so important in our prison system today.

Just as I was heartbroken and worried about my children, thousands of other incarcerated moms are as well. They go through the same hurts I did. Many are angry, grieving, and desperately seeking peace and a place to find comfort. But with the opportunity to come together with other moms going through the same things, lifting up their children in prayer, they can discover the peace God has for them. God is just waiting to pour out His blessing on each of us—even those whose wrong choices resulted in separation from children and family.

I have experienced these blessings most through answered prayer. When I came together in prayer with other mothers, God heard my petitions. He answered them and by this He taught me that I could trust in Him. I am so grateful to be back with my family now and hold my children in my arms. It is my dream to, one day, bring Moms In Touch into our local prison system. I want to offer these women hope, so they too can experience the peace and joy of God's mercy and grace that I came to know.

Pray Together

[Jesus said,] "If you believe, you will receive whatever you ask for in prayer."
—Matthew 21:22

Dear heavenly Father,
I lift up all the incarcerated mothers who are worried about their children. I ask that You would comfort them and bring them peace. I pray that moms across the country and world would take Moms In Touch into prisons so these women can have hope and know You in a deeper way. May they come to know the promises and the love You have for them and their children, and may You restore their lives. In Your Son's precious name, amen.

May the peoples praise you, O God;
    may all the peoples praise you.
Then the land will yield its harvest,
    and God, our God, will bless us.
                    —PSALM 67:5-6

———————

God has chosen to rule the world by prayer.
             —WESLEY DUEWEL, *Touch the World Through Prayer*

CHAPTER TWENTY-FOUR
Taking MITI to Ethiopia
by Kathleen Wendeln of California

On the other side of the world, Pastor Yoseph Menna and his wife, Ribca, were praying. The director of 8,500 Ethiopian churches had discovered a ministry called Moms In Touch International, and he desperately wanted to give his country the vision of praying for its children and schools. He and his wife knew how much Ethiopia's children need prayer. They need prayer for safety, for health, for protection. And for salvation.

Yoseph, a vibrant Ethiopian, knew that, more than anything else, his beloved African country needs to bring mothers together to pray passionately for their children and schools. He and his wife saw the importance of having the *Moms In Touch International Booklet* in their language, Amharic, so women could read for themselves about praying scripturally, surrounded by other moms helping them lift their burdens to the Lord. The couple prayed big prayers, asking God to supply the $10,000 needed to print ten thousand booklets they wanted in Amharic. Soon, the answers to their prayers came tumbling in. One mom in the United States donated the entire amount!

But these faithful prayer warriors didn't stop there. They weren't praying just for the booklet; they were also praying that longtime Moms In Touch moms would come to Ethiopia to train women in the Four Steps of Prayer. They prayed that God would provide the training sites, and that the Ethiopian moms would be excited to participate in the training.

BEING PART OF AN ANSWER TO PRAYER

I was privileged to be part of an answer to prayer, along with 19 other Moms In Touch women who flew to Ethiopia in July 2007. Our adventure half-way around the world was a direct answer to the prayers of Yoseph and Ribca.

In the middle of a rainy night, after 22 hours on a plane, we landed in the heavily guarded Ethiopian airport. Yet our long trek from the United States was nothing compared to the journey the Ethiopian moms would be making to participate in our training sessions. They trudged through muddy, slippery roads—some walking a day and a half to get there. Others traveled on crowded buses. These precious moms were eager to hear about focused prayer for their children and schools. A team of Ethiopian women, whose passion for the Lord pours from them, had worked hard planning and preparing 14 different training sites and inviting the women to attend.

The Ethiopian leadership had set up seven training sites in Addis Ababa, the capital city, and seven more in another city. They divided us into groups of three to lead each session.

Our first day of training began with a one-and-a-half-mile trek in the rain. The bus we were on couldn't make its way through the muddy, rain-soaked roads. So the driver got us as close as he could to the church, but then we had to walk. As we walked up to the church, we were delighted to hear the women worshiping the Lord in song. Inside the church, we could see the joy radiating from their faces as they praised our God Almighty in their own language.

SHARING MITI WITH ETHIOPIAN MOMS

When we spoke we used a translator, and we always began by showing a globe to illustrate that MITI was in more than 120 countries. We also pointed out Canada, where Fern Nichols started Moms In Touch, and then Poway, California, where Moms In Touch International has its headquarters. We also brought a mat to illustrate the story of Jesus healing the paralyzed man in Luke 5:17–26 and to show how MITI moms join together in one-accord prayer, putting our children one at a time "on the mat" to lift our cares and concerns to the Lord. If one mom tries to carry her child all by herself, it is too much. She can become discouraged. But with a woman on each corner of the mat carrying the child to God, the burden is lighter.

The women then had the opportunity to symbolically place their children on the mat and bring them to Jesus. Seeing the glimmer of hope coming into each of the mom's eyes was something that touched me. These women were mighty prayer warriors, but, as mom after mom told us, they were happy to learn how to focus their prayers for each of their children, praying in groups of twos and threes for specific needs. They wanted to ask God to shape their children's character and direct their children's futures. How exciting to think that the prayers for this youngest generation might impact the future of Ethiopia.

In many countries, Moms In Touch groups encourage the school staff through a program called "Words and Deeds." We had prayed about how to share the idea of "Words and Deeds" with the Ethiopian moms, and we were thrilled to hear the response from the women. We explained that many times our teachers often hear the complaints and rarely "thank you" from the parents. The Ethiopian moms began to share that they also were guilty of complaining about the teachers and blaming them if their children faced difficult situations. However, they began to see that God would rather parents pray for teachers, thank them, and show them appreciation. Many of the Ethiopian moms were excited about this idea and shared how they were going to thank their children's teachers through notes or small gifts such as flowers.

A TIME TO CELEBRATE

After the day-and-a-half training session, with 50 to 100 ladies at each location, we all gathered together for a joy-filled, boisterous celebration. We had a powerful time of rejoicing with our "sisters in Christ" from halfway around the globe. These moms were so thankful that God had used us to answer their prayers.

One sweet elderly woman told us, "I praise God for how He taught us this different way to pray, and to pray for the next generation. I now have a purpose to live: to keep praying!" Another mom said, "You are an answer to our prayers. We have been praying for our children just when they are older and have problems. We did not know we should pray for our small children, and for God's blessing on their lives ahead."

We were honored to meet two dear women who traveled from Kenya to join us for the training. There are many MITI groups in their area, and they were excited to learn more to share with the other women. They both helped with the training and then shared in the celebration time with their testimonies. In Addis Ababa, one of these moms shared, "My dear sisters, the hand of God and these moms from the United States have united the hands of the women from Kenya with the women of Ethiopia. This is a miracle to us. We are moms united in prayer for one common thing: the children. In these last days it is so timely to pray. Don't take the life of a child for granted. We have been praying alone for years. Thank you to the founder and our sisters from America. Do not get tired!"

A God-Sized Answer

Yoseph and Ribca had been praying that many Ethiopian women would learn about MITI. God, again, answered their prayers in surprising ways. All in all, nine hundred moms were trained. But little did we know that message would have a ripple effect throughout Ethiopia. Our last training session was videotaped and broadcast via TV to 20 million!

However, the story doesn't end there. Just four months later, more than 1,300 Ethiopian groups had started. The following year, Moms In Touch leadership in Ethiopia helped train two thousand more women, with five hundred more groups starting. God has heard the cries of their hearts, and is answering their prayers. Ethiopian moms have shared their excitement about seeing God at work, changing their country one child at a time. Moms share that they continue to see many changes in their children, both spiritually and physically, as a result of God answering their prayers. One mom wrote to say, "One of my children was always sick. We prayed in MITI and this child is now free from all diseases. Before, we didn't know how to pray for our children's sexual relationships or how to protect them; now we are praying not only for this but also for their marriages. We are also seeing relationships among the women grow, which we had not seen before."

One MITI group in Ethiopia reports they asked God to provide the opportunity for their heavily Muslim area to hear about Christ's saving grace. Not long after, the church-planting ministry e3 Partners presented the gospel in that area, and 230 Ethiopians became Christians! God is not only changing the lives of their children and their schools, but He is also transforming their communities by bringing more to Him.

Blessed to Be Used by God

The 20 moms from the United States who traveled to Ethiopia for the training were blessed as well. "Ethiopians may be poor financially, but they are extremely rich spiritually," said one of the trainers. "We learned much from them. Some have been persecuted and imprisoned for their faith. We saw many people on the streets accept Christ after women in our group shared the gospel. Each one of us came away changed by what God had shown us through our time with the Ethiopian moms."

Yoseph and Ribca have been blessed, too, watching the answers to their prayers tumble in. Nearly two thousand groups of women are meeting regularly around Ethiopia pleading with God for the spiritual and physical lives of their children and schools. They wait in tiptoe anticipation to see how their prayers will impact this generation, their country, their region, and perhaps even the world.

Pray Together

[Jesus said,] "Ask and it will be given to you; seek and you will find; knock and the door will be opened to you. For everyone who asks receives; he who seeks finds; and to him who knocks, the door will be opened."

—MATTHEW 7:7–8

Dear Lord Jesus,
Sustain moms around the world. Give hope to those living in desperate situations. Remind them that You are a God who loves them and cares for them. Gather them together to pray for their children and schools and answer their prayers in mighty ways. May they always wait with expectation for You to move among their community. In Your name, amen.

Call upon me in the day of trouble;
I will deliver you,
     and you will honor me.

               —PSALM 50:15

———

To pray is nothing more involved than to open the door, giving Jesus access to our needs and permitting him to exercise His own power in dealing with them.

              —DR. OLE HALLESBY, *Prayer*

Chapter Twenty-Five
HOPE FOR MOMS OF PRODIGALS
by Barbara Schneider of California

IN HIS GROWING-UP YEARS, MY SON MARK'S SPIRITUAL LIFE WAS UP AND DOWN. WHEN HE ATTENDED CHURCH CAMP HE CAME HOME EXCITED ABOUT JESUS. BUT WITHIN A WEEK OR SO OTHER INTERESTS TOOK PRIORITY AGAIN. UNTIL HIS JUNIOR YEAR OF HIGH SCHOOL.

That year, his love for God and the Bible kept growing even in the months following camp, and I thought things were finally going to be different. He shared scriptures with friends and remained active in church and the Christian club at school throughout the school year.

That summer, my husband, Vic, said he had accepted Jesus as his Savior. Mark and my daughter, Jennifer, were so excited. They gave their dad a beautiful Bible for his birthday, and I was thrilled. At last, our whole family was committed to following the Lord Jesus!

Yet sadly, it was short-lived. My husband put the Bible down after a few weeks. And when Mark's senior year of high school began, he and his best friend turned their backs on God (citing hypocrisy in the church as their reason). Mark left youth group and started hanging out with a sketchy crowd. My thin, six-foot-tall son grew his brown hair long and would have gotten piercings, but his dad laid down the law about that as long as he was under our roof. As his life took a turn to the dark side, Mark started wearing only black clothes, drinking and partying, even growing marijuana in our home.

My heart was broken.

Through all this, I continued to pray in my Moms In Touch group. However, it became a real struggle, as most of the other moms were focusing prayer on which university their child should attend. My son had adamantly decided *not* to go to college. I began to wonder if I still had a place in the group, but I desperately needed the support of other women to pray for my son.

STARTING A PRAYER GROUP FOR "PRODIGAL" CHILDREN

That fall at a MITI rally, several moms spoke of praying for "prodigal children," those who had wandered away from God. Hearing this gave me an idea. I started a Moms In Touch group with a friend whose son had also decided that Christianity wasn't worthwhile. Other moms and an aunt joined us, and each week we poured out our hearts in prayer for the spiritual and physical lives of our teen prodigals.

Focusing on attributes of God filled us with hope. One of my favorites during that time was the sovereignty of God. Meditating on that part of God's nature reminded me that He was completely and perfectly in control of Mark's life and mine—no matter how things looked! Nothing could happen to either of us outside His plan. God could bring about circumstances in Mark's life that would bring him to a complete turnaround, and God could keep Mark physically alive until then.

God consistently led us to just the right scriptures to pray, such as the Old Testament verse Jeremiah 24:7 (NASB). I often prayed that verse, inserting my son's name: "I will give [Mark] a heart to know Me, for I am the LORD; [Mark will be one of] My people, and I will be [Mark's] God, for [Mark] will return to Me with [his] whole heart."

We realized that seeking God's Holy Spirit to draw each of these boys back to their loving heavenly Father is a *total and lifelong commitment*, so we asked for perseverance to keep praying. We did not want halfhearted boys, but men who were sold out to God. Thus, we asked God to do *whatever* He needed to do in their lives to bring them to Him, pleading that He protect them from death alone, until they made that commitment.

GOD'S PROTECTION

God was so gracious in protecting our boys physically. The first year out of high school Mark moved to Lake Tahoe to work at a ski resort. Early in the season during maintenance work on a deck, rotten wood was being discarded into barrels. Mark knew the barrels were to be burned, so he lit a match and tossed it into one of the barrels. What he didn't realize was that the barrel also contained gasoline. In the resulting explosion Mark received only a slight burn on his hand and a few singed hairs. He could have been killed.

When he came home for a visit, I thought perhaps God might have gotten through to him, but nothing had changed spiritually. He had grown longer hair and a beard and was sporting a nose ring and a tongue ring; he later added two lip rings. That same winter two famous individuals perished in skiing accidents, running into trees. Mark also hit a tree while going off a snowboard jump. His friends saw him and thought surely they would be carrying his lifeless body down the hill, but he injured only his knee. And it wasn't even broken! I sensed God's hand of protection was with Mark in both of these accidents as a result of our prayers for him.

God continued to protect Mark through several automobile accidents in which vehicles were totaled, yet he and his friends were never seriously injured. In all Mark's extensive travels, God has kept him safe through many near misses. Only He knows from how many others my son has been spared.

Mark returned home from Lake Tahoe unmotivated to get a full-time job or go to school. He worked evenings delivering pizza, partied all night, and slept all day. We prayed for motivation, and the first totaled car provided that incentive. (You can't deliver pizza without a vehicle.) He started to learn a little responsibility, working a full-time day job and keeping his part-time evening job for over a year—not leaving much time to party.

PERSEVERING

We moms continued to pray, although nothing was changing in Mark's life. Many a tear was shed, but there were always arms of comfort and prayers for strength. After a few years, one of our group member's sons returned to God and completely gave his life to Him. What a breakthrough and encouragement to the rest of us!

Meanwhile, Mark began seeking truth, first looking into other religions. However, he found nothing to commit himself to. Gradually, he was led to the inescapable conclusion that Jesus is in fact the one true way to God. But he was not ready to get off his road to ruin. At the same time, Mark began to realize that God was answering my prayers, so when his friends needed help or healing, he would ask me to pray for them. Occasionally, I would even see his Bible out in his room.

As is our custom in Moms In Touch, we always prayed that our children would be caught when doing wrong. God blessed us with answers. The biggest was Mark's driving under the influence (DUI). He was naturally upset with being caught, but he accepted his guilt and paid the price without grumbling.

RECOGNIZING ANSWERS TO PRAYER

Once when he and several friends were driving to Lake Tahoe for a long weekend of snowboarding, I mentioned that I'd pray that it would not snow. Because they were traveling at night, I was worried about dangerous ice conditions. Mark came completely unglued and screamed, "Mom, you can't pray for no snow. Please don't pray for no snow!" I agreed to pray only for their safety on the roads, but for the first time I knew that Mark had become convinced that God is real, and that He loves to answer my prayers and those of my MITI friends.

Mark began to take a greater interest in music. He was taking lessons and needed a guitar. We'd thought about getting him an inexpensive one for Christmas but hadn't seriously looked. Then one evening after work, Mark asked me, "Have you been praying for a guitar for me?"

"Well, no, I really haven't, though we thought about getting you one for Christmas."

Then he showed us a $2,500 guitar that his best friend's father had given him, saying that God told him to give the guitar to Mark. Even though the father had argued with the Lord, God insisted, and the man was obedient. This sacrificial gift made a huge impact on Mark.

In the spring of 2000, my daughter, Jennifer, worked for a travel agency that was planning a cruise called "Footsteps of Paul," sponsored by my church. Many pastors would be teaching along the way. Jennifer and I both wanted to go and, after praying, we asked my husband and son if they would like to join us. They were both excited and all four of us signed up.

In spite of Mark's long hair, beard, and body piercings, several of the pastors quickly made friends with him. Aboard ship, the pastors taught the books written to the particular cities we were to visit and the letters to the churches in Revelation. The teaching to the church at Ephesus about leaving your first love was the message that touched Mark's heart. After seven years in a destructive lifestyle, he surrendered his life completely to Jesus that day in Turkey.

Following that commitment, Mark continued to grow in his faith. He was active in church, attended Bible college classes, and looked forward to continuing his service on the mission field, with a focus on India.

After Bible college, he attended evangelism school. Upon graduation, he founded a missions ministry with his friend called S.E.N.D. Ministries (Serving and Evangelizing Nations in Despair). The ministry sends out teams of six to ten missionaries to work alongside native pastors and missionaries for five months to spread the gospel. S.E.N.D. has sent many teams to India, Israel, Morocco, and Costa Rica. Countless seeds have been planted in these countries and people have come to faith in Christ.

Mark—my once prodigal son—and his coworkers have seen thousands come to Christ and have helped plant several churches. There have been numerous miraculous healings—both physical and spiritual—and the team members have returned home more aware of the power of God.

While ministering in India, Mark shared with pastors that his mom was involved with Moms In Touch. That sparked interest and subsequently, the MITI ministry was asked to come and hold a conference in Bangalore, India. In 2004, I was able to travel there with another woman from the ministry and talk with 135 women about the blessing of praying for children and schools. As a result of that conference, there are now many mothers praying together in Bangalore, and the word of Moms In Touch is spreading to other areas of India.

ON THE MISSION FIELD

Four years ago, Mark married Joy, the daughter of a pastor he worked with in India, and they now have a one-year-old daughter. His desire to equip believers to be "sent out" and his vision to minister the gospel to oppressed people around the world continue to grow.

How grateful I am that God not only brought my son back to faith in Him, but also gave Mark a heart for the nations and sent him to serve, disciple, and send others to mission fields so that countless people can hear the gospel, have an opportunity to know Christ, and spend eternity with Him.

God did and continues to do exceedingly abundantly *more* than we could have ever wished for, prayed for, or imagined in my son's life when we began praying as a small group of moms with prodigal children.

Pray Together

I will give them a heart to know me, that I am the Lord. They will be my people, and I will be their God, for they will return to me with all their heart.

—JEREMIAH 24:7

Almighty, sovereign Lord, in whom nothing is impossible,
We bring before You our sons and daughters whose hearts are far from You. We ask that You turn their lives around, so their hearts are sold out for You. Use the circumstance of their lives to bring them to a wholehearted commitment to You. In Your powerful name, amen.

HOW TO KNOW THAT GOD WILL HEAR YOUR PRAYERS
AN EXCERPT FROM *PRAYERS FROM A MOM'S HEART* BY FERN NICHOLS

Just as a mom recognizes the voice of her own child, so the heavenly Father knows the voice of each one of His children. If you have a question or doubt concerning your relationship with God, let me share with you how you can be certain you are His child.

Think about this unshakable truth: God loves you personally! In His great love He gave the world His greatest treasure—His only child, Jesus Christ. Jesus died on the cross in your place as payment for your sins and for the sins of the whole world. Because of His death and resurrection, you can experience God's indescribable love, both now and throughout all eternity.

No matter where your sins have taken you, God's forgiveness is perfect and complete because of the sacrifice of His Son. Will you take your first step of faith by believing in your heart that Jesus died for you and rose from the dead to give you eternal life? If you accept Him into your life as Savior and Lord, you will never be the same. He can replace your loneliness, fears, frustrations, and guilt with His love and forgiveness. He also promises to hear your prayers and answer them with all the delight of an earthly parent responding to the desires of a much-loved child.

Make the following scriptures and prayer the first and most important prayer of your life as you begin praying for your children.

Pray Alone or Together

If you confess with your mouth, "Jesus is Lord," and believe in your heart that God raised him from the dead, you will be saved. For it is with your heart that you believe and are justified, and it is with your mouth that you confess and are saved.

—ROMANS 10:9-10

To all who receive [Jesus], to those who believe in his name, [God] gave the right to become children of God.

—John 1:12

Dear Father,
Thank You for sending Your Son, Jesus, to die on the cross for my sin.
I want to be Your child. Please come into my heart and forgive me of all my sins.
I want to live for You alone.
Thank You for making my heart Your home.
In Jesus' name, amen.

If you have sincerely prayed this prayer, you are a member of God's family. You are His child! You now can know for sure that God will hear and answer your prayers.

Welcome to the Family of God!

NOTES

Chapter Nine: A Divine Heart Transplant

1. Elisabeth Elliot, *Shadow of the Almighty: The Life and Testament of Jim Elliot* (New York: Harper, 1958), 132.

Chapter Fifteen: My Heart Still Sings

1. Carl Sandburg, "Losers," *The Complete Poems of Carl Sandburg* (Boston: Houghton Mifflin, 2003), 189.
2. See the New Testament passage Ephesians 6:10-19 for more on the subject of spiritual warfare.
3. E. M. Bounds, *Purpose in Prayer* (Grand Rapids: Revell, 1920), 9.
4. Oswald Chambers, *My Utmost for His Highest* (New York: Dodd, Mead & Company, 1963), 211.

More Great Resources
from Focus on the Family®

Experiencing God Around the Kitchen Table
by Marilynn Blackaby & Carrie Blackaby Webb

Pull up a chair and have a seat at the kitchen table of someone who has faced life's blessings and its trials. Marilynn Blackaby has often been asked about the challenges of raising five children while her husband, Henry, was heavily involved in ministry and frequently away from home. With grace and humor, Marilynn weaves in lessons she's learned over the years as she shares her personal stories. Marilynn's experiences and wisdom will bring hope and encouragement to your heart.

Losing Control & Liking It
by Tim Sanford, M.A.

It's been drummed into your head: You have to make your kids turn out right. If you don't, what will people think? Worse, what disasters await if your child takes the wrong path? The truth is that you can't make your kids turn out right. It's not even your job. In fact, your real role as a parent is much more rewarding, pleasant, and doable. Let experienced counselor and parent Tim Sanford show you how to give up your fears about your teenager's future—and the control you never really had. You'll discover the truth about how God parents His children, and it will set you free.

The Mom You're Meant to Be
by Cheri Fuller

Motherhood is meant to be a blessing, not a burden. So why do so many moms seem exhausted and frustrated? Moms can get so busy that they often miss out on the best moments of motherhood. *The Mom You're Meant to Be* urges moms to forget the formulas and lean on God's wisdom to raise their children. You'll be energized and encouraged by the wisdom of this book, which captures what it means to be a mom.

OR MORE INFORMATION

Online:
Log on to FocusOnTheFamily.com
In Canada, log on to focusonthefamily.ca.

Phone:
Call toll free: 800-A-FAMILY
In Canada, call toll free: 800-661-9800.

BPZZXP1